HUMAN RIGHTS AND PERSONS WITH DISABILITIES IN CAMEROON

HUMAN RIGHTS AND PERSONS WITH DISABILITIES IN CAMEROON

ROLAND DJIEUFACK
YUH ANTOINETTE

GALDA VERLAG 2025

Bibliografische Information der Deutschen Nationalbibliothek
Die Deutsche Nationalbibliothek verzeichnet diese Publikation in der Deutschen Nationalbibliografie; detaillierte bibliografische Daten sind im Internet über https://dnb.de abrufbar.

ISBN 978-3-96203-456-6 (Print)
ISBN 978-3-96203-457-3 (E-Book)

DEDICATION

To our families

PREFACE

The primary objective of this book is to raise the general awareness of the respect of the human rights of persons with disabilities in Cameroon. Persons living with disabilities are a group of persons that are vulnerable because disability comes with so many challenges such as discrimination and violence within the society, family and institutional settings. This study aims at pointing out the hurdles that beset the enforcement of the rights of persons with disabilities in Cameroon from a human right-based approach. In an attempt to establish this fact, this study strongly notes that persons with disabilities in Cameroon are most often marginalized and their rights are frequently violated. This is compounded by the fact that mindful of their rights which are enshrined across different international and domestic statutes, the effective protection of their rights as prescribed under Cameroonian Law in particular is a call for concern.

Adopting both qualitative and quantitative research methodology, involving in-depth content analysis of primary and secondary data, this study advocates for an enhanced enforcement of the laws in place in order to adequately guarantee and enforce the human rights of persons with disabilities in Cameroon. The emphasis today in Cameroon in particular, is towards the respect of dignity and welfare of persons with disabilities through the effective implementation of the human rights instruments. By the findings registered by this study, persons with disabilities in Cameroon are incessantly complaining of being marginalized in different sectors of the society through neglect, stigmatization and disrespect. Despite the existence of legislations governing the rights of persons with disabilities in Cameroon, there is still an urgent need for stakeholders concerned with the conditions of persons with disabilities to adequately exercise their responsibilities; and it is in response to this duty that this book has been written. This is clearly an indication that Cameroonians particularly those living with disabilities are becoming more conscientious and that the Cameroonian government is, to some extent, responding adequately to their preoccupations. In this book, the authors have carefully discussed their viewpoints from a legal perspective drawn purely from a human right basis. This current study is a clear reflection of the efforts put in by the authors during years of Doctorate research as we have drawn from existing literature on human rights law in general in Cameroon as well as from other jurisdictions, analyzed the relevant statutes and elucidated on material drawn from extensive field research work conducted in Cameroon.

The book is in five chapters. Chapter One opens up with a general introduction. Chapter two discusses the concept of persons with disabilities. Chapter three presents the nature of the rights of persons with disabilities as a vulnerable group in Cameronn. Chapter four discusses the regulatory mechanisms protecting the rights of persons with disabilities in Cameroon. Chapter five highlights the challenges to the enforcement of the rights of persons with disabilities in Cameroon. Chapter six concludes by presenting the findings and convincing suggestions on this subject.

The book is a useful source of reference for students of Human right law, legal practitioners, magistrates and judges, social workers who actively are involved in the welfare of persons with disabilities. This study will definitely go a long way to enhance understanding to existing regulations on persons with disabilities in Cameroon.

Roland Djieufack, Ph.D
Yuh Antoinette, Ph.D
Cameroon

ACKNOWLEDGEMENTS

This study indeed would not have been conducted without the assistance of many persons who in various ways aided to shape our ideas. We actually had the assistance of some staff working in the decentralized services of the Ministry of Social Affairs, Ministry of Women's Empowerment and the Family, Ministry of Vocational Training and Employment, Ministry of Higher Education, Ministry of Basic Education found in the major cities of Bamenda, Buea, Douala and Yaoundé in Cameroon. We also register our gratitude to some associations concerned with persons with persons with disabilities, especially the staff and stakeholders of the *Mbingo Baptist Disability Centre* in Bamenda, and the *Rehabilitation* Institute for the blind -BULU Centre in Buea, Cameroon for responding positively to our questions and provided useful information. We are thus confident that our findings will be a great importance to the stakeholders involved in the welfare of vulnerable groups in Cameroon. We humbly accept and take responsibility for all errors and omissions in this book.

Roland Djieufack, Ph.D
Yuh Antoinette, Ph.D
Cameroon

CONTENTS

LIST OF LEGAL INSTRUMENTS

National Instruments

a) Laws

- The 1983 Law on the Protection of People with Disabilities.
- The 1998 Education Framework Act, No. 98/004.
- Law 004/022 regulating the provision of private education.
- The Southern Cameroon High Court Law 1955.
- Law No. 1968-LF-3 of the 11th June 1968 to set up the Cameroon Nationality Code.
- Law No. 83/13 of 21 July 1983, relating to the protection of persons with disability.
- Law No. 90/1516 of 26 November 1990, binding the modalities of application of law 83/13 of 21st July 1983, relating to the protection of persons with disability.
- Law No 96/06 of the 18th of January 1996 relating to the Constitution of Cameroon.
- Law No. 2004-16 of July 22, 2004 on the creation, organization and functioning of the National Commission for Human Rights and Freedoms.
- Law No. 2010/002 of 13 April 2010 Relating to the Protection and Welfare of Persons with Disabilities.
- Law No. 2016/007 of July 12, 2016, relating to the Penal Code.
- Law No. 2019/005 of 25April 2019 to amend and supplement some provisions of Law No. 2012/01 of 19 April 2012 relating to the Electoral Code.

b) Decrees

- ☐ Decree of 2000 instituting free Primary Education.
- ☐ Decree 75/467 of 28 June 1975 creating the Ministry of Social Affairs Cameroon.
- ☐ Decree No 76/460 of October 12, 1976 relating to Military Pensions.
- ☐ Decree 78/056 of 23 February 1978 establishing the National Rehabilitation Centre for the Handicapped (CNHR).
- ☐ Decree 80/199 of 9 June 1980 creating the National School for Social Affairs Workers (ENAAS) Yaounde.
- ☐ Decree No. 90-1459 of 8 November 1990 establishing the National Committee for Human Rights and Freedoms.
- ☐ Decree No.90/1516 of November 26, 1990 laid down modalities for the implementation of the 1983 Law on the Protection of People with Disabilities.
- ☐ Decree No. 2009/096, 16 March, 2009 Operationalizing the National Centre for the Rehabilitation of Persons with Disabilities.
- ☐ Decree No. 2018/6233/PM of 26th July 2018 Fixing the Procedures for the Application of Law N° 2010/002 Of 13 April 2010 on the Protection and Promotion of Persons with Disabilities in Cameroon.

c) Orders and Circulars

- ☐ Joint circular 34/06/LC/MINSEC/MINAS of 2 August 2006 to ensure free access to secondary education for PWDs.
- ☐ Order No. 040/PM of 19 May 2022 to lay down terms and conditions for granting age exemption to persons with disabilities during competitive examinations and recruitment into public service.

Regional Instruments

- ☐ African Union Convention for the Protection and Assistance of Internally Displaced Persons in Africa (Kampala Convention) 2009.
- ☐ African Youth Charter, 2006.
- ☐ Regional Convention on the Recognition of Studies, Certificates, Diplomas, Degrees and other Academic Qualifications in Higher Education in the African States 1981.
- ☐ The African Charter on Human and Peoples' Rights 1981.
- ☐ The African Charter on the Rights and Welfare of the Child 1990.

- ☐ The African Charter on the Rights and Welfare of the Child 1990.
- ☐ The OAU Refugee Convention 1969.
- ☐ The Protocol to the African Charter on Human and Peoples' Rights on the Rights of Women in Africa 2003.
- ☐ The Protocol to the African Charter on Human and Peoples' Rights on the Rights ofPersons with Disabilities in Africa 2018.

International Instruments

a) Laws and Covenants

- ☐ Universal Declaration of Human Rights (UDHR) 1948.
- ☐ Constitution of the World Health Organization. Geneva, World Health Organization, 1948.
- ☐ International Covenant on Economic, Social, and Cultural Rights (ICESCR) 1966.
- ☐ The International Covenant on Civil and Political Rights (ICCPR), 1966.
- ☐ The International Covenant on Civil and Political Rights 1966.
- ☐ Principles for the Protection of Persons with Mental Illnesses and the Improvement of Mental Health Care (1991).
- ☐ Charter on Inclusion of Persons with Disabilities in Humanitarian Action 2016.

b) Conventions and Treaties

- ☐ The Medical Examination of Young Persons (Industry) Convention, 1946 (No. 77).
- ☐ Medical Examination of Young Persons (Non-Industrial Occupations) Convention, 1946.
- ☐ The Employment Service Convention (No. 88) 1948.
- ☐ The Geneva Conventions 1949.
- ☐ The UN Refugee Convention 1951.
- ☐ The Convention relating to the Status of Refugees, 1951.
- ☐ International Labour Organisation Convention No. 102 of 1952.
- ☐ International Labour Organisation Social Security Convention 1952.
- ☐ The ILO Discrimination (Employment and Occupation) Convention 1958.
- ☐ UNESCO Convention against Discrimination in Education 1960.

- The International Labour Organization's 1962 Convention No. 117 concerning Basic Aims and Standards of Social Policy.
- The International Convention on the Elimination of All Forms of Racial Discrimination (ICERD), 1965.
- International Labour Organisation Invalidity, Old-Age and Survivors' Benefits Convention 1967.
- The ILO Human Resources Development Convention, 1975.
- The Convention on the Elimination of All Forms of Discrimination against Women (CEDAW), 1979.
- International Labour Organisation (ILO) Vocational Rehabilitation and Employment (Disabled Persons) Convention 159 of 1983.
- The Convention Against Torture and Other Cruel, Inhuman or Degrading Treatment or Punishment 1984.The International Labour Organization's 1989 Convention No. 169 concerning Indigenous and Tribal Peoples in Independent Countries.
- Convention on the Rights of the Child 1989.
- UNESCO's Convention on Technical and Vocational Education, 1989.
- The Convention on the Protection of the Rights of All Migrant Workers and Members of Their Families (CRMW) 1990.
- The International Convention on the Protection of the Rights of All Migrant Workers and Members of Their Families (ICRMW), 1990.
- Anti-Personnel Mine Ban Convention 1997.
- Convention on Conventional Weapons (CCW) 1981 as amended in 2001.
- United Nations Convention on the Rights of People with Disabilities 2006.
- Convention on Cluster Munitions 2008.
- Marrakesh Treaty on the facilitation of Access to Published Works for Persons Who Are Blind, Visually Impaired or Otherwise Print Disabled, 2013.

c) Declarations

- UN Declaration on the Rights of Mentally Retarded Persons, 1971.
- Declaration on the Rights of Deaf-Blind Persons, 1979.
- The Jomtien Global Declaration on Education for All, 1990.
- The Vienna Declaration, 1993.
- The Salamanca Declaration of 1994.
- Copenhagen Declaration, 1995.

- ☐ Beijing Declaration on the Rights of People with Disabilities, 2000.

d) Recommendations

- ☐ The Workmen's Compensation (Minimum Scale) Recommendation, 1925 (No. 22).
- ☐ The International Labor Conference (ILC) Recommendation No. 71 in May 1944.
- ☐ Medical Examination of Young Persons Recommendation, 1946 (No. 79).
- ☐ The Employment Service Convention Recommendation (No. 83), 1948, concerning the organization of employment services.
- ☐ International Labour Organisation Vocational Rehabilitation (Disabled) Recommendation 1955.
- ☐ The Recommendation against Discrimination in Education (1960).
- ☐ The Recommendation concerning the Status of Teachers (1966).
- ☐ The Recommendation concerning Education for International Understanding, Cooperation and Peace and Education relating to Human Rights and Fundamental Freedoms (1974).
- ☐ The Recommendation on the Development of Adult Education (1976).
- ☐ The ILO Vocational Rehabilitation and Employment Recommendation 168 of 1983.
- ☐ The Recommendation on the Recognition of Studies and Qualifications in Higher Education (1993).
- ☐ The Recommendation concerning the Status of Higher-Education Teaching Personnel (1997).
- ☐ The Revised Recommendation concerning Technical and Vocational Education and Training (2001).

e) Resolutions and Non-binding instruments

- ☐ International Labour Organisation resolution on Vocational Rehabilitation of Disabled People 1965.
- ☐ The Standard Rules on the Equalisation of Opportunity for Person with Disabilities 1993.
- ☐ United Nations Security Council Resolution S/RES/2475(2019).

Foreign Instruments

- European Convention on Human Rights, 1950.
- American Convention on Human Rights, 1969.
- The United Nations Standard Rules on the Equalisation of Opportunities for Persons with Disabilities 1993.
- The Nigerians with Disability Act 1993.
- The Rights of Persons with Disabilities Act of India, 2016.

LIST OF CASES

De Wilde, Ooms and Versyp v Belgium (1970) 1 EHRR 373.

Del Rio Prada v Spain (2014) 58 EHRR 37 at [125] Dupin v. France, no. 2282/17, Decision of 19 Dec. 2018.

Free Legal Assistance Group and others v. Republic Democratic of Congo Comm. No. 25/89, 47/90, 56/91, 100/93.

H M v Switzerland [2002] 1 MHLR 209.

HL v the United Kingdom (2005) 40 EHRR 32.

Nielsen v Denmark (1988) 11 EHRR 175.

Ranjit Kumar Rajak v. State Bank of India, 5 Bom. C.R., 227 (2009).

Social and Economic Rights Action Center and the Center for Economic and Social Rights v. Nigeria (communication No. 155/96).

Storck v Germany [2005] 1 MHLR 211.

Western Cape Forum for intellectual Disability v Government of the Republic of South Africa & Another 2011 5 SA 87 (WCC).

ABBREVIATIONS/ACCRONYMS

ADP	African Disability Protocol
API	Additional Protocol I
APII	Additional Protocol II
Art.	Article
CAT	Convention Against Torture and Other Cruel, Inhuman or Degrading Treatment or Punishment
CCM	Convention on Cluster Munitions
CEDAW	The Convention on the Elimination of All Forms of Discrimination against Women
CERD	Committee on the Elimination of Racial Discrimination
CESR	Committee on Economic, Social, and Cultural Rights
Chap.	Chapter
CNHR	National Rehabilitation Centre for the Handicapped
CRC	Convention on the Rights of the Child
CRPD	Convention on the Rights of Persons with Disabilities
ECHR	European Court of Human Rights
EFA	Education for All
ELECAM	Elections Cameroon
ENAAS	National School for Social Affairs Workers

ESCR	Economic, Social and Cultural Rights
HRC	Human Rights Committee
ICCPR	International Covenant on Civil and Political Rights
ICESCR	International Covenant on Economic, Social, and Cultural Rights
ICF	International Classification of Functioning
ICRC	International Committee of the Red Cross
ICRMW	International Convention on the Protection of the Rights of All Migrant Workers and Members of Their Families
IE	Inclusive Education
IHL	International Humanitarian Law
IHRL	International Human Rights Law
ILC	International Labour Conference
ILO	International Labour Organisation
MDGs	Millennium Development Goals
NCHRF	National Commission on Human Rights and Freedoms
NRCPD	National Rehabilitation Center for People with Disabilities
NSIF	National Social Insurance Fund
OHCHR	Office of the High Commissioner for Human Rights
OUA	Organisation African Unity
POW	Prisoners of War
PWDs	Persons with Disabilities
SDGs	Sustainable Development Goals
Sec.	Section
UDHR	Universal Declaration of Human Rights
ULD	Universal Learning Design

UN CESCR	United Nations Committee on Economic, Social and Cultural Rights
UN	United Nations
UNAPHAC	National Union of Cameroon Associations of Persons with Disabilities
UNCRPD	United Nations Convention on the Rights of Persons with Disabilities
UNESCO	United Nations Educational, Scientific, and Cultural Organization
UN-HABITAT	United Nations Human Settlement Program
UNHRC	United Nations Human Rights Commission
UNHRP	United Nations Housing Rights Programme
US	United States
WHO	World Health Organisation
WPA	World Program of Action

CHAPTER ONE

GENERAL INTRODUCTION

1.0 Background of the Study

Historically, persons with impairments or disabilities have suffered systematic discrimination and exclusion from national issues including issues that directly affect their lives. Negative perceptions about persons with disabilities and their subsequent placement in confined institutions, increased their exclusion from mainstream society, thus limiting their ability to integrate in society and make their voices heard on many issues including sports, politics, education etc. Although efforts at protecting and promoting the rights of persons with disabilities started years ago it is suggested that the United Nations (UN) Declaration of 1981 as the International Year for Disabled Persons marked a major turning point in the lives of persons with disabilities. This declaration provided leverage for persons with disabilities who realised the need to mobilize themselves both at the national and international levels to make their voices heard on injustices against them.[1]

Approximately one billion people, 15% of the global population experience some form of disability, with 110 -190 million experiencing significant disability. These persons face disproportionate socio-economic marginalization, resulting in poorer health and medical treatment, lower quality education, limited employment prospects and generally broad- ranging restrictions on their community participation. Persons with impairments face

1 Okupua P. Maxwell, Mprah K. Wisdom, and Saka N. Bernard, (2016), "Participation of persons with disabilities in political activities in Cameroon" Disability and the Global South, Vol.3, No. 2, p. 981.

significant levels of discrimination and are often prevented from participating in their communities. This exacerbates their plight and thus necessitates the quest for the protection of their rights. The fact that PWD's can be frequently prevented from enjoying their basic human rights by persons with whom they interact further demands and justifies their lawful protection.[2]

Studies indicate that a majority of persons with disabilities experience social marginalisation and deprivation, and are excluded from many socioeconomic activities. For example, it has been indicated that, on an average, and as a group, persons with disabilities are more likely to experience adverse socio-economic conditions such as lower educational attainment, poorer health outcomes, lower employment, and higher rates of poverty than persons without disabilities. As a consequence, persons with disabilities are more likely to have limited access to safe housing, food, and health-care, jobs etc.[3]

The social model of disability acknowledges that obstacles to participation in society and its institutions reside in the environment rather than in the individual, and that such barriers can and must be prevented, reduced or eliminated. Environmental obstacles come in many guises and are found at all levels of society. They are reflected in policies and regulations created by governments. Such obstacles may be physical for example barriers in public buildings, transportation and recreational facilities. They may also be attitudinal widespread underestimation of the abilities and potential of PWDs creates a vicious cycle of under expectation, under-achievement and low priority in the allocation of resources.[4]

At the international scene, there exists the much-heralded Universal Declaration of Human Rights and the 2006 Convention on the Rights of Persons with Disabilities. Nationally, there exists a surfeit of laws for the protection of the rights of PWD's. These laws include, *inter alia,* the 1996 Cameroonian Constitution,[5] and the 2010 Law Relating to the Protection and Welfare of

[2] Awa Rumarick., (2021), "The Protection of the Rights of Persons with Disabilities (PWDs) in Cameroon: Prospects and Challenges," pg. 1 at https://hrlrc.org/2021/06/17/the-protection-of-the-rights-of-persons-with- disabilities-pwds-in-cameroon-prospects-and-challenges/

[3] Opokua P. Maxwell, et al, (2016) "Lives of persons with disabilities in Cameroon after CRPD: voices of persons with disabilities in the Buea Municipality in Cameroon" International Journal on Disability and Human Development, p. 1 at: https://www.researchgate.net/publication/302978914 (accessed on the 20th of February 2022)

[4] Innocenti Research Centre, (2007), "Promoting the Rights of Children with Disabilities", at www.unicef-irc.org (accessed on the 20th of February 2022).

[5] Law No 96/06 of the 18th of January 1996 relating to the Constitution of Cameroon

Persons with Disabilities.[6] Cameroon has become the second African country to begin to ratify the African Disability Protocol (ADP), which addresses unique issues and discrimination that affect people with disabilities living in African countries.[7] The president of the Republic of Cameroon has also signed and ratified the UN's Convention on the Rights of Persons with Disabilities (CRPD), which aims to protect the rights of and transform attitudes towards people with disabilities.

The rights of persons with disabilities are not new rights *per se*, rather, they bring poignancy to human rights that already exist but have been historically denied or marginalized. The challenges and impediments faced by persons with disabilities in Cameroon are significant and should therefore not be treated with levity. Consequently, the Cameroonian legislator has hitherto enacted a plethora of laws and set-up commendable institutional mechanisms for the protection of this category of persons. However, a critical examination of these laws and their actual fulfilment reveals a yearning gap between legal theory and practical reality. This is so evident as we find the rights of persons living with impairments continuously not guaranteed in many aspects, for instance, limited rights to education, jobs, accessibility to public and private buildings and social welfare places.[8] From a field trip in the cities of Buea and Bamenda in Cameroon, there exist some private owned rehabilitation and educational training centers catering for the welfare of children with disabilities concerned with the vocational training of children with disabilities such as carpentry, catering, sewing, etc. Notwithstanding the efforts of such centres, the treatment relating to the access or state of training of some children with impairments in some public and private schools is relatively slow and deplorable.[9] In fact, this situation does not reflect an

---

6 The Law No. 2010/002 of 13 April 2010 Relating to the Protection and Welfare of Persons with Disabilities.

7 The protocol was adopted by the African Union in 2018, and enables countries to draw up disability laws and ensures citizens are able to hold their governments to account. Mali has already adopted the protocol, but it will only come into force once it has been ratified by 15 member states of the African Union.

8 The authors conducted thirty-three interviews in the cities of Cameroon namely; Buea, Bamenda, Bafoussam, Dschang and Yaounde. The interviewees included: ten pupils; ten University students, three legal practitioners, seven senior bureaucrats in the Ministries of Social Affairs, Basic Education, Secondary Education, Higher Education and Vocational Training, and five centres concerned with persons with disabilities. One officer was interviewed in Elections Cameroon (ELECAM); the study in charged with elections in Cameroon. The authors also interviewed two officers in the UN based system in Yaounde. The officers interviewed in the government institutions and UN structure was done by telephone while systematic fieldtrips were made in the aforementioned cities.

9 The University of Bamenda in Cameroon in 2008 has made a commendable effort in enacting an

effective implementation of the provisions of Section 3 of Chapter 3 of Law No. 2010/002 on the protection and advancement of people with disabilities which allows for special education for people with disabilities in Cameroon.[10]

Regrettably, the existence of adoption and implementation of international, regional and national substantive and procedural measures for their protection, and notwithstanding the energy, zeal and actions envisaged in the application of these laws, there is a persistent violation of the rights of persons with disabilities at various instances in Cameroon.[11] Monitoring violation against the rights of the elderly with disabilities in particular has actually been a problem.[12] This is exacerbated by the fact that normative gaps, informative gaps and implementation gaps are very conspicuous from a reading of these instruments. These gaps have actually left the socio-legal rights of persons with disabilities adequately unprotected under Cameroonian law.

Another angle of the problem stems from age discrimination and ageism are widely tolerated across the world. Negative ageist attitudes towards old age and older people with impairments in Cameroon are deeply ingrained in many societies and, unlike other forms of prejudice and discriminatory behaviour, are rarely acknowledged or challenged. This has led to widespread marginalization of persons with impairments and is at the root of their isolation and exclusion.

Irrespective of all the programs put in place to protect disable persons in law, this group of persons have remained largely neglected. Disable people are the world's largest growing minority, yet until very recently they were invisible in the international human rights law. Persons with disabilities face discrimination and barriers that barr them from participating in society

implementation policy for the enhancement of the rights of education of students with disabilities. As a rule, practical measures are adopted each academic year to ease the admission of some candidates with disabilities into some classical and professional programs. In spite of this, there are some concerns raised by some students with disabilities complaining about their difficulties in accessing toilets, offices and lack of a special corner for them in classrooms. This problem is further compounded in some private secondary schools where proper measures do not exist in catering for the rights of students with disabilities because of lack of adequate finances.

10 This Law guarantees the rights of children and adolescents with disabilities in having access to education and exempting them from school fees for public school programs.

11 Awa Rumarick., (2021), *Op.cit*, p. 2

12 The researcher attended workshops organized by the Baptist Health Centre in Bamenda in 2022 and 2023. Discussions during these gatherings reveal that the rights of persons with disabilities not fully respected different sectors in the society. Sylvia B. Ambang, *Socio-Legal Protection of the Vulnerable Group under International Law: Case Study of the Elderly*, Ph.D. Thesis, University of Soa, Faculty of Law and Political Science, (Unpublished), P. 8.

on an equal basis with others every day. Persons with disabilities have, however remained largely invisible, often sidelined in the rights debate and unable to enjoy all the full range of human rights.This discrimination often includes physical or mental disability in various aspects such as employment participation in sports and other abilities. There's therefore a need for the law to enforce these rights.

Substantively, this work is specifically on the rights of persons with disabilities in Cameroon specifically from a human right perspective. We therefore make use of national, regional and international pieces of legislations that protect the rights of PWDs. As such, its geographical sphere is Cameroon and per time, we are looking at these rights with respect to the present decade.

CHAPTER TWO

THE CONCEPT AND TYPES OF PERSONS WITH IMPAIRMENTS

2.0 Introduction

Before a legally binding Convention on the rights of persons with impairments can be framed, the category of persons entitled to those rights must be defined. First of all, there is no single paradigm for persons with disabilities or physically challenged persons, both of which relate to a multi-faceted process that is determined not only by the passage of time, but also by physiological, social and cultural factors.

A distinction has to be made between the chronological aspects of persons with disabilities and its social construct. According to the chronological criterion used by a majority of the countries in the America, European, Asian and African regions in their legislation, persons with disabilities occur regardless of the age or sex, although this threshold has changed more in recent years than at any other time in the entire history of the Western world.

The chronological definition of age is determined by socio-cultural factors. As each society sets an age limit after which people are considered to be part of the older or elderly population, persons with disabilities affect either the youth or the old and is closely related to physical or physiological factors. In general, the state of disability is correlated with the loss of certain instrumental and functional capacities that are required to maintain a person's autonomy and independence and, although this will vary from individual to individual, it is directly related to the normative definitions which a culture ascribes to changes in the body.

Disability can thus be both a time of loss and a time of fullness, depending on the combination of individual and generational resources and opportunities to which people have access during their lives. This, in turn, will be determined by their situation and their position within society. Disability thus combines with other factors of social differentiation such as gender, social class and ethnic origin in determining a person's access to those resources and opportunities and the person's ability to take advantage of them.

In addition, the various approaches to the interpretation of the issues addressed by laws, policies and programs for persons with disabilities must be identified. The issues dealt with by these types of instruments are social constructs that reflect specific world views[13] and are directly related to the concept of physical dysfunctions that serve as the basis for the delineation of approaches for achieving given objectives.

Traditionally, the predominant view, at a programmatic level, of physically challenged persons have characterized it as a stage at which economic, physical and social capacities are all declining. In the first case, this is reflected in reduced income; in the second, in a loss of autonomy; and, in the third, in the absence of a social role. The rights-based approach paves the way for a paradigm shift in this regard, since it promotes the empowerment of persons with disabilities and the creation of a physically integrated society. This implies that persons with disabilities are subjects of law and not simply beneficiaries; they therefore enjoy certain guarantees and are endowed with responsibility towards themselves, their family and society, their immediate surroundings and to future generations[14].

These considerations all form part of the debate concerning physically challenged persons or persons with disabilities as public and human rights issues on today's international and regional policy agendas.

2.1 Concept of Persons with Impairments

Aging is typically defined as the chronological age, which is the number of years, months or days that have elapsed from birth. Many gerontologists

---

13 Sandra H.and Rodríguez-Piñero L., (2015) "*Ageing and the protection of human rights: current situation and outlook*" *IusGentium Comparative Perspectives on Law and* Justice, Volume 45.

14 Charles D. E. and Roger W. C., (1993), "Agenda setting and Policy: Strategies and agenda denial", *Policy Study Journal*, volume 21 issue 1 March.

believe definitions of aging that focus exclusively on calendar time are incomplete because they are independent of physiological, psychological and socio-cultural factors. They also believe that to increase our understanding of senescence, other measures of aging designed to differentiate among individuals of the same chronological age are needed. These measures are often described as indices of functional age, which include physiological, psychological and social age. A definition of the concept of old age can be approached from at least three different standpoints based on chronological, physiological and social factors.

Biological age research typically focuses on senescent changes, biological or physiological processes and their subsequent effect on behaviour. A common goal is used to determine relative age, or the extent to which an individual is aging faster or slower than an average person of the same chronological age. For example, an individual who is aging successfully and exercising regularly may have a biological age 10 years younger than his or her chronological age. Conversely, a person experiencing multiple medical problems in old age may be biologically older than they are chronologically[15].

With physiological aging, most systems exhibit structural and functional declines. These disruptions in the integrity of the cell are, in turn, precursors of more gross morphological changes, such as decreased elasticity and compliance, demyelization and neoplastic growth. As expected, these structural changes are almost always associated with profound behavioural consequences.

Social age refers to the concept that society often has fairly rigid expectations of what is and is not appropriate behaviour for a person of a particular age. The impact of social roles and expectations on the lifestyle choices of older people is of considerable interest in experimental gerontology.

2.1.1 Chronological Concept of Persons with Impairments

Chronological age is a key quantitative variable that has been exploited by demographers since a link between mortality and age was first established more than three centuries ago.[16] That it is used as a variable of choice for the analysis of all demographic phenomena suggests that chronological

[15] Morgan E. L and Eileen M. C., (2019) "Is 60 the new 50? Examining changes in Biological Age over the past two-decades",*PMC Journal National Institute of Health US National Library of Medicine.*

[16] Séguy, I. et al, (2019), *Chronological age, social age and biological age*, 10.13140/RG.2.2.28706.68801. Institut national d'etudes demographiques.

age is the determinant of all demographic behaviours.[17] However, while the notion of age as the time that elapses between a person's birth and the phenomenon under study appears obvious to us today, it may encompass a number of different realities, depending on the individual, the time and the place concerned. Chronological age is essentially biological in nature and is manifested in differing degrees of various functional disorders. It refers to age as measured in years. When this criterion is used, old age is defined as beginning at 60 or 65 years and is often set by law for "older adults" or "senior citizens". From this standpoint, ageing entails changes in a person's place within society, since many responsibilities and privileges especially those associated with employment are determined by his or her chronological age.[18] The ageing process is of course a biological reality which has its own dynamic, largely beyond human control. However, it is also subject to the constructions by which each society makes sense of old age. In the developed world, chronological time plays a paramount role. The age of 60 or 65, roughly equivalent to retirement ages in most developed countries is said to be the beginning of old age. In many parts of the developing world, chronological time has little or no importance in the meaning of old age. Other socially constructed meanings of age are more significant such as the roles assigned to older people; in some cases, it is the loss of roles accompanying physical decline which is significant in defining old age. Thus, in contrast to the chronological milestones which mark life stages in the developed world, old age in many developing countries is seen to begin at the point when active contribution is no longer possible.

Physiological factor is determined by the physical process, which, although linked to chronological age, cannot be equated directly with a person's age as measured in years. This definition of age relates to the loss of functional capacities and the gradual decline in bone density, muscle tone and strength that occur with the passage of time.[19]

One of the terms associated with physiological age is "senility", which refers to the physical and/or mental deterioration experienced by some people which prevent them from continuing to lead a normal social and private life[20]. Other

---

17 Ibid Pg 10.

18 Sera A, and Gin J, (1995), *Connecting gender and aging: A Sociological Approach Buckingham and Philadelphia*, Open University Press.

19 Ibid, p. 5.

20 Sandra Huenchuana nd Luis Rodríguez-Piñero Ageing and the protection of human rights: current situation and outlook *Economic Commission for Latin America and the Caribbean (ECLAC)* Alejandro Vicuña Leyton LC/W.353 Copyright © United Nations, March 2011. All rights reserved.

related terms are the "old-old" (a minority group composed of weak and sickly persons) and the "young-old" (older persons who, despite their chronological age, are vital, vigorous and active)[21]. Human evolution suggests that the default position for health is to be physically active. Inactivity, by contrast, has serious negative effects on health across the lifespan. Therefore, only in physically active people can the inherent aging process proceed unaffected by disuse complications. In such individuals, although the relationship between age and physiological function remains complex, function is generally superior with health, wellbeing, and the aging process optimized.

2.1.2 Social Concept of Persons with Impairments

The sociology of ageing has developed numerous ways of looking at and interpreting the social positions of older persons. The major theoretical approaches to this sort of analysis are the functional theory on ageing, the political economy of ageing and the theory of structural dependency.

Advocacy of the functional theory perspective is disengagement theory, which suggests that withdrawing from society and social relationships is a natural part of growing old. There are several main points to the theory. First, because everyone expects to die one day, and because we experience physical and mental decline as we approach death, it is natural to withdraw from individuals and society.[22] Second, as the elderly withdraw, they receive less reinforcement to conform to social norms. Therefore, this withdrawal allows a greater freedom from the pressure to conform.[23] Finally, social withdrawal is gendered, meaning it is experienced differently by men and women. Because men focus on work and women focus on marriage and family, when they withdraw, they will be unhappy and directionless until they adopt a role to replace their accustomed role that is compatible with the disengaged state.[24] This approach to old age characterizes it as a detachment from society and, in terms of game theory, as a progressive loss of functionality. The critics of this approach argue that this way of looking at ageing provides an ideological tool for justifying characterizations of the ageing population as problematic and

---

Printed at United Nations, Santiago, Chile.

21 Diane E. P, (1988), *Human Development* New York : McGraw-Hill 155 PAP.

22 *Cumming* E. and *Henry* W., Growing Old: The Process of Disengagement. Basic Books, New York, *1961*. (Reprint: Arno, New York, 1979, ISBN 0405 118147).

23 Ibid. pg 16.

24 Cumming, E. and Henry, W. (1961), *Growing Old: The Process of Disengagement.* Basic Books, New York.

unproductive members of society who are not committed to its development. Though being aged, the elderly still contribute to the development of every society. Without the elderly to guide the younger generation to be protective in the society, we will be facing a society full of unproductive youths. They also point up the emphasis that it places on each person's situational adaptation, which opens the way for the development of a growing sense of egocentrism and isolation during old age[25].

In terms of the political economy of ageing, the key point in understanding the position of older people in modern capitalist society is that their quality of life during this stage in the life cycle is directly influenced by the individual's position in the labour market at the time he or she retires[26]. Critics of this approach argue that, although it may be a useful one, the fact is that a pre- and post-retirement continuum does not exist, at least in the economic sphere (income level) or in terms of social (work-based) relations; they also point out, however, that the alternative - that of considering older persons as a homogeneous social category of persons uninvolved in the production system who do not pay social security taxes - is not satisfactory either[27].

Structural dependency theory directs attention towards the overall social system rather than the characteristics of given persons. Structured dependency is often seen to cross over with political economy in the literature.[28] The theory comes from a conflict perspective, which tries to address the role that older people have been "forced" into and explores what brings about isolation and depression, as created by the processes of Disengagement theory. It has a sociological background and provides evidence that ageing is of social construction. Social context is of great importance in explaining the basis for how this theory was developed, and why it largely comes from a Macro-level perspective. It focuses on the role an action of the state and society in creating a dependent older population,

---

25 Ageing and the protection of human rights: current situation and outlookSandra Huenchuan and Luis Rodríguez-Piñero Economic Commission for Latin America and the Caribbean (ECLAC) Alejandro Vicuña Leyton LC/W.353 Copyright © United Nations, March 2011. All rights reserved. Printed at United Nations, Santiago, Chile.

26 International Journal of Health Services; The Aging Enterprise: in whose Interest Carroll. L Estes April 1, 1986. https:/doi.org/10.2190/XHXV-RTAV-RCFL-5JEN.

27 Ageing and the protection of human rights: current situation and outlook Sandra Huenchuanand Luis Rodríguez-Piñero Economic Commission for Latin America and the Caribbean (ECLAC) Alejandro Vicuña Leyton LC/W.353 Copyright © United Nations, March 2011. All rights reserved. Printed at United Nations, Santiago, Chile.

28 Peter, T. (1980),*The Structured Dependency of the Elderly: A Creation of Social Policy in the Twentieth Century*, Volume 1, Issue 1, Cambridge University Pres.

through retirement, pensions and residential care. The government's actions influence where the elderly stand in society, and the public perception of ageing. It asserts that the structure and organization of the production sector is at the root of dependency and runs counter to approaches that emphasize social constructions[29].

This last theory sheds light on important issues, particularly with respect to the standards and resources that influence and place limitations on the day-to-day lives of older persons. It also sets aside the individualism of earlier theories on ageing[30]. However, none of these theories questions the assumptions underlying the mainstream school of thought, which looks at people's lives within the context of established sociological frameworks and measures older persons against the standard of the productive and reproductive lives of younger generations[31]. None of this provides a satisfactory basis for understanding old age.

In short, the models used for looking at the status and position of older persons in society have been based on biomedical and social perspectives that are anchored in the past and that, for the most part, have portrayed this group as a problem for their families and society and have characterized ageing as an obstacle to development. This view of old age and ageing is used to segregate older persons and to keep them at a distance.

Thus, all the entryways to the structures of daily life - the workplace, the family, social interactions- are based, for the most part, on the prevailing "standard", which, in this case, are people of working age. Viewed from this perspective, chronological age is the main source of physical problems, declining functionality, economic difficulties or a lack of appreciation for the roles of older adults. Thus, the fact that older persons are not integrated into society is seen as being their fault, rather than society's. It was not until the 1980s that, thanks to the United Nations' efforts, the analysis of the problems faced by older persons and possible solutions began to be addressed within the context of the debate concerning the public sector and the welfare State. This was acknowledged in the decision reached by the World Assembly on the Elderly in 1982 to change its name to the World Assembly on Ageing "in

---

29 Nicos, P. M. (1991), *Back to Sociological Theory of Construction of social Orders*, St. Martin's Press.

30 Sandra Huenchuanand Luis Rodríguez-Piñero Ageing and the protection of human rights: current situation and outlook Economic Commission for Latin America and the Caribbean (ECLAC) Alejandro Vicuña Leyton LC/W.353 Copyright © United Nations, March 2011. All rights reserved. Printed at United Nations, Santiago, Chile.

31 Toni, M. C. and Kathleen F. S., (2001), *Gender, Social Integrities, and Aging* Altamira Press A Division of Rowan and Littlefield Publisher, Inc 1630 North Main Street.

view of the interrelatedness of the issues of aging individuals and the aging of populations."[32].

Clearly, then, although persons with disability is necessarily biological and chronological, the most important aspect from a human-rights perspective is its social construct. In developed society, the existing view of persons with disabilities and the issues of concern to them focuses on the idea of physical dysfunction as a stage during which persons will have unmet economic, physical and social needs[33]. As a result, many of the policies and actions relating to persons with disabilities focus on what other groups have that they do not, based on an androcentric organizational and functional model of the society.

The predominant focus of policy measures, by their very nature, is on mitigating these losses or shortfalls, and they are often designed only for those individuals and sectors that rely on the State for subsistence. Only in rare cases is government action focused on offering the highest possible living standards for persons with disabilities based simply on their identity as members of society and on their legitimate aspirations as citizens. The reason for this is that government institutions have not yet adapted either structurally or ideologically to the shift in the age distribution of the population. They continue to operate on the basis of a youth-centered construct in which physical inappropriateness is invariably associated with loss[34].

Persons with disabilities are viewed in terms of the extent to which they approach or depart from a supposed standard of normality that, far from being neutral, is clearly biased in favour of physical and mental parameters that fit in with the dominant culture's stereotype[35]. The situation is even more difficult for older persons with disabilities, who are often viewed through the prism of established paradigms, many of which simply disregard age relations.

Under these circumstances, discrimination can be said to be the greatest problem facing persons with disabilities, in as much as it interferes with or blocks the recognition, enjoyment or exercise, on an equal footing, of all fundamental political, economic, social, cultural, civic and other human rights and freedoms. As a corollary, persons with disabilities are exposed to

---

32 Resolution 35/129 on problems of the elderly and the aged, 92nd plenary meeting, 11 December 1980.

33 Huenchuan Navarro: *Aging, human right and public policies* worldCat Identity Conference papers and proceedings.

34 Ibid. P. 3

35 Serah E. Curtis; Health and Inequality (2004). DOI:< https://dx.doi.org/10.4135/9781849209243>

poverty and a lack of visibility and are placed in an increasingly untenable position, with all of these situations taking on the particular characteristics associated with this stage of life.

Clearly, the formal recognition of equal rights as set forth in existing international human rights instruments or national laws, with no further distinction being made, does not adequately redress the disadvantageous position in which persons with disabilities currently find themselves, since the prevailing structure and ideology prevent this from occurring. Some countries do have laws and regulations that encourage persons with disabilities to participate fully in society, but they often fail to achieve their purpose because the surrounding environment does not facilitate the full exercise of their rights as citizens. Society segregates them from other age groups, and older persons, as a group, also tend to act as a sector that has little influence in the corridors of power, all of which perpetuates their unbalanced position in terms of the distribution of resources and benefits generated by the development process.

A person with disability is invariably associated with a loss of capacity. Older persons with disability for example may be viewed as having returned to a childhood state in which their age renders them incapable of being independent. They are not thought of as citizens, or at least not active ones, but rather, in the best of cases, as simply dependents who, by virtue of that position, receive certain social benefits. And although steps may be taken to enhance given individual skills or capabilities (relating to, for example, leadership or participation), they are rarely fully incorporated into relevant spheres of action[36].

A person with disability therefore has limited scope in which to exercise their equality and freedom owing to the existence of explicit inequalities in terms of their status or position and their rights and to the fact that public policies often fail to take their needs into account[37]. It should be recognized, however, that persons with disability are not the only ones that face this kind of problem. At different points in time, other social groups like old age persons have also voiced the same concerns.

Consequently, in the cases of women, children and persons with disabilities, these concerns have led to the adoption of specific human rights instruments whose purpose have been to reaffirm the applicability

---

[36] Sandra Huenchuanand Luis Rodríguez-Piñero*Ageing and the protection of human rights: current situation and outlook Economic Commission for Latin America and the Caribbean (ECLAC)* United Nations, March 2011. Printed at United Nations, Santiago, Chile.

[37] United Nation Human Development Report Report 1995.

to those groups of rights that are more generally recognized in other international instruments. Examples include the Convention on the Elimination of All Forms of Discrimination against Women (1979), the Convention on the Rights of the Child (1989) and the Convention on the Rights of Persons with Disabilities (2007). This has not been the case with older person, impliedly authorizing some degree of discrimination against them.

2.1.3 Biological Concept of Persons with Impairments

The approach taken to biological concept of persons with disabilities is based on two theories: the theory of programmed ageing, according to which the ageing of the body is part of a normal developmental pattern for each type of organism that is predetermined for each species and is subject to no more than minor modifications; and the theory of natural "wear and tear", according to which the body ages due to its continuous use, i.e., age is the result of cumulative damage to the body[38].

Proponents of the theory of programmed ageing argue that, because each species has its own pattern of ageing and life expectancy, this pattern is set and innate, whereas advocates of the wear-and-tear theory compare the body to a machine whose parts ultimately wear out after long use[39].

The difference between the two theories has practical implications. If people are programmed to age in a certain way, little can be done to slow the process and ward off dependency. Consequently, all older persons are dependent. By contrast, if people age because their bodies are wearing out, then there is something they can do to shield them from physiological stress, increase their life expectancy and improve their quality of life.

By the same token, some gerontologists draw a distinction between "primary ageing" (the gradual process of physical deterioration that begins at an early age and continues, inexorably, as the years pass) and "secondary ageing" (the result of illness, abuse and other factors that, in many cases, are under a person's control)[40]. The distinction between primary aging, representing innate maturational processes, and secondary aging, representing the effects of environment and disease was used to

---

38 Diane E. P, (1988), *Human Development* New York : McGraw-Hill 155 PAP.

39 Ibid.pg 2.

40 Ibid.Pg 3.

develop a model for the assessment of factors that are associated with age-related individual differences in intelligence.[41] Intelligence was measured by performance on a number of tests that measure cognitive abilities known to decline with age. In a hierarchical multiple regression analysis, primary aging and education but not health explained a significant portion of the variance in fluid intelligence.[42]

Chronological age had a residual effect over and above that of primary and secondary aging, indicating that there was remaining age-associated variance unaccounted for in the proposed model. The results suggest that the model of primary and secondary aging is a valid means of operationalizing chronological age.

2.1.4 Psychological Concept of Persons with Impairments

This perspective focuses on the individual and the way in which he or she copes with the passage of time. Growing older, viewed from this vantage point, is seen as a personal process of adaptation to the changes both in the body and in one's social environment that occur as a person age. In analytical terms, the emphasis is on the ways in which individuals confront and respond to the changes that they undergo, how they seek solutions for the problems they face, and how they accept and assume the losses that will inevitably come so that they can continue to feel content and interested in life[43]. Psychological age is how old one feels, acts, and behaves, and is thus not necessarily equal to chronological age, which is age since birth. A person can therefore have a psychological age that exceeds their chronological age if they are mature or at least feel older than they really are.

This approach has been criticized for relying too heavily on generalizations based on certain characteristics that are assumed to be exhibited by everyone at given stages in the life cycle[44] and for not taking due account of the social dimensions of ageing and, as a result, viewing older persons as a homogenous group with the same needs, skills and forms of behaviour.

---

41 Kaarin, A. et al, (1994),"Primary Aging, Secondary Aging, and Intelligence", *Psychology and Aging*, Vol 8. Pages. 562-570.

42 Ibid.Pg 2.

43 Sandra Huenchuanand Luis Rodríguez-Piñero Ageing and the protection of human rights: current situation and outlook Economic Commission for Latin America and the Caribbean (ECLAC) United Nations, March 2011. All rights reserved. Printed at United Nations, Santiago, Chile.

44 Ibid.

One of the concepts associated with this school of thought is that of "successful ageing"[45], which is described as the result of the maintenance of functional, physical, mental, emotional and social capacities, good nutrition, an active or engaged lifestyle and recourse to suitable means of compensating for declining skills, among other elements[46].

According to the theory about maintaining an active life, the more active the older population is, the more successfully the members of that population will age[47]. A different concept of successful ageing is developed in the theory of disengagement, which characterizes ageing as a mutual process of distancing. Older people voluntarily cut back on their activities and commitments, while society promotes generational segregation by pressuring older persons to retire and to withdraw from social and other activities. Some critics of this theory assert that this disengagement is more closely associated with factors such as poor health, widowhood, retirement and impoverishment than with age as such[48].

This approach also encompasses the theory which associates this stage of life with the eighth psychosocial crisis in the development of the ego: "ego integrity versus despair"[49]. If integrity wins out, it paves the way for wisdom described as an informed and detached concern with respect to life versus death. The other side of the picture is disheartened apathy as a reaction to a growing sense that the end is growing near and of confusion and helplessness.[50]

Psychosocial theory contends that industrialized societies tend to foster discouragement and, as its correlates, apathy, rather than ego integrity or wisdom.[51] This theory points out that, in traditional rural societies, the paradigm for the resolution of this crisis is provided by older persons and is based on the application of their accumulated knowledge and skills to decision-making and daily life. In sum, it is based on wisdom (also understood as the

---

45 Stephen, K, (2015). "Critical Perspectives on Successful Aging", *Oxford Journal, The Gerontologist,* Feb, vol. 5, issue 1, pages. 26-33.

46 Martha R. C, et al, (2002), "Rowe and Kahn's Model of Successful Aging Revisited: Positive Spirituality- The Forgotten Factor", *The Gerontologis,* volume 42, issue 5, October, pages, 613-620.

47 Diane E. P, (1988), *Human Development* New York : McGraw-Hill 155 PAP.

48 Ibid.Pg 4.

49 Syeda, F. T and Sarah. S, (2014), "Relationship between Ego, Integrity, Despair, Social Support and Health Related Quality of Life", *Pakistan Journal of Social and Clinical Psychology,* Vol. 12, No. 1. Pages, 26-33.

50 McLeod, S. A. (2018, May 03). *Erik erikson's stages of psychosocial development.* Simply Psychology.

51 Huenchuan Navarro: *Aging, human right and public policies*worldCat Identity Conference papers and proceedings.

pragmatic expression of intelligence), which enables older persons to look at their capacities and limitations and which helps them to choose wisdom as the path for resolving this final life crisis.

2.2 Types of Impairments

2.2.1 Vision impairment

Vision impairment refers to people who are blind or who have partial vision. When talking with a person who is blind or has a vision impairment. Visual disabilities can range from mild or moderate vision loss in one or both eyes to substantial or complete loss of vision in both eyes. Some people experience reduced or lack of sensitivity to certain colors or color blindness, as well as sensitivity to brightness. These include:

- Color blindness - difficulty distinguishing between colors generally red and green, or yellow and blue, and sometimes the inability to perceive any color.
- Low vision - includes blurry vision, seeing only the middle of the visual field, seeing only the edges of the visual field, and clouded vision.
- Blindness - substantial loss of vision in both eyes.

2.2.2 People who are deaf or hard of hearing

Hearing impairments can range from mild to profound. People who are hard of hearing may use a range of strategies and equipment including speech, lip-reading, writing notes, hearing aids or sign language interpreters.

When talking to a person who is deaf or hard of hearing:

- look and speak directly to them, not just to the people accompanying them, including interpreters
- speak clearly and use a normal tone of voice unless otherwise instructed by the person with the hearing impairment
- if you don't understand what a person is saying, ask them to repeat or rephrase, or alternatively offer them a pen and paper

2.2.3 People with mental health conditions

Mental illness is a general term for a group of illnesses that affect the mind or brain. These illnesses, which include bipolar disorder, depression, schizophrenia, anxiety and personality disorders, affect the way a person thinks, feels and acts. A person with a mental health condition may experience difficulty concentrating, which can sometimes be a result of medication. Try to avoid overly stressful situations wherever possible so that their condition is not exacerbated.

2.2.4 People with Intellectual Impairments

A person with an intellectual disability may have significant limitations in the skills needed to live and work in the community, including difficulties with communication, self-care, social skills, safety and self-direction. The most important thing to remember is to treat each person as an individual:

- a person with an intellectual disability is just like everyone else - treat them as you would like to be treated
- be considerate of the extra time it might take for a person with an intellectual disability to do or say something
- be patient and give your undivided attention, especially with someone who speaks slowly or with great effort

2.2.5 People with acquired brain injury (ABI)

Acquired brain injury (ABI) refers to any type of brain damage that occurs after birth. The injury may occur because of infection, disease, lack of oxygen or a trauma to the head. Around 160,000 Australians have some form of acquired brain injury, with more men affected than women. The long term effects are different for each person and can range from mild to profound. It is common for many people with ABI to experience:

- increased fatigue (mental and physical)
- some slowing down in the speed with which they process information, plan and solve problems
- changes to their behaviour and personality, physical and sensory abilities, or thinking and learning

- may also have difficulty in areas such as memory, concentration and communication

A person with an Acquired Brain Injury does not have an intellectual disability and does not have a mental illness.

2.2.6 People with Autism Spectrum Disorder

Autism is an umbrella description which includes Autistic disorder, Asperger's syndrome and atypical autism. Autism affects the way information is taken in and stored in the brain. People with autism typically have difficulties in verbal and non-verbal communication, social interactions and other activities. Impairments usually exist across three main areas of functioning:

- social interaction
- communication, and
- behaviour (restricted interests and repetitive behaviours)

Many people with an autism spectrum disorder also have sensory sensitivities, that is; over or under sensitivity to sight, touch, taste, smell, sound, temperature or pain. Those with Asperger's syndrome are typically of average or above average intelligence, and can show a wide range of behaviours and social skills. People with Asperger's syndrome may display some of the following characteristics:

- difficulty in forming friendships
- ability to talk well, either too much or too little, but difficulty with communication
- inability to understand that communication involves listening as well as talking
- a very literal understanding of what has been said. For example, when asked to 'get lost', as in go away, a person with Asperger's syndrome will be confused and may literally try to 'get lost'
- inability to understand the rules of social behaviour, the feelings of others and to 'read' body language. For example, a person with Asperger's syndrome may not know that someone is showing that they are cross when frowning
- sensitivity to criticism

- a narrow field of interests. For example, a person with Asperger's syndrome may focus on learning all there is to know about cars, trains or computers
- eccentricity

2.2.7 People with Physical Impairment

The common characteristic in physical disability is that some aspect of a person's physical functioning, usually either their mobility, dexterity, or stamina, is affected. People with physical disability are usually experts in their own needs, and will understand the impact of their disability.

There are many different kinds of disability and a wide variety of situations people experience. The disability may be permanent or temporary. It may exist from birth or be acquired later in life. People with the same disability are as likely as anyone else to have different abilities.

2.3 The Perception of Persons with Impairments from a Human Rights-Based Approach

The world is aging, and this demographic shift necessitates social workers with gerontological knowledge and expertise. The physiological, social and economic changes that commonly impact persons with disabilities and frequently contribute to dependency make them vulnerable to having their human rights violated. By focusing on needs rather than rights, the human dignity, security, and autonomy of the individual can be easily ignored. As people become physically challenged, they encounter transitions that affect all areas of their lives. Retirement often means changes in relationships as well as economic status. Widowhood and the loss of closed relatives and friends can induce intense feelings of grief that can be numbing without skilled and sensitive interventions. Physical changes can limit mobility, while mental impairment can impede overall functioning. Such changes frequently impact relationships as traditional roles are altered. Consequently, changing family structures mean that persons with disability are often left with limited support. A critical consequence of these life changes that is often overlooked is the impact that they have on the human rights of persons with disability.

Subsequent to the Universal Declaration of Human Rights, several special conventions were adopted by the General Assembly of the United Nations focused on specific population groups including the Convention on the Elimination of All Forms of Discrimination against Women, the Convention on the Rights of the Child, Convention on the Protection of the Rights of All Migrant Workers and Members of their Families, and the Convention on the Rights of Persons with Disabilities. Countries ratifying conventions are legally bound to adhere to their standards.

At its thirty-first session the Economic Commission for Latin America and the Caribbean in March 2006, (ECLAC) stated that: "Given the principle that public policy must be guided by a rights-based approach, development processes should be pursued within the normative, substantive and procedural framework of civil, political, economic, social and cultural rights as set forth in binding national and international agreements."

These perspectives alter the assumptions underlying the development of laws, policies and programs, since the point of departure is no longer the provision of assistance to people who have certain needs, but rather the existence of persons with certain rights which the State and the rest of society must uphold[52]. Member states are therefore the main subject of development, and the universal guarantees set forth in the international community's human rights system constitute a conceptual framework capable of informing a coherent set of guiding principles and rules ECLAC, 2006. This approach also provides a way of setting out States' obligations in terms of respect for the economic, social, cultural, civil and political rights involved in any long-term strategy.

2.4 Conclusion

This chapter reveals the various concepts of persons with disabilities and upholds the justification of their rights. All these concepts, which are the chronological, physiological, and social aging clearly highlight the fact that physical disability is inevitable and at some point in everyone's life, we might incur a disability. Chronological concept of aging refers to age as measured in years. As concerns physiological concept of aging, age is determined by the physical aging process this is associated with physical and mental deterioration. Social concept of refers to the attitude and behaviour that comes with the state of disability. Although physical inability necessarily entails a biological and

---

52 United Nations Human Rights Office of the High Commissioner for Human Rights Annual Report 2006.

chronological interpretation, the most important aspect from a human-rights perspective is its social construct. In Western society, the prevailing view of persons with disability and the issues of concern to them focuses on the idea of disability as a stage during which persons will have unmet economic, physical and social needs[53]. As a result, many of the policies and actions relating to such persons focus on what other groups have that they do not, based on an androcentric organizational and functional model of society.

To date, the Cameroonian legislator has enacted a convention on the rights of people with disabilities. Equally, the human right-based approach of such persons are spread across different conventions and treaties making it difficult to fully ensure the protection of the legal rights of persons with disabilities. At this point, it will be of relevance for us to study an assessment of the effectiveness of the existing regulatory frameworks on the protection of the rights of persons with disabilities under Cameroonian law.

---

53 Huenchuan Navarro: *Aging, human right and public policies*worldCat Identity Conference papers and proceedings

CHAPTER THREE

CHALLENGES FACED BY PERSONS WITH DISABILITIES THAT HINDER THE EFFECTIVE ENFORECEMENT OF THEIR RIGHTS IN CAMEROON

3.0 Introduction

Though the types of violations of the rights suffered by people with impairments and other disadvantaged groups can sometimes be compared, it is crucial to emphasize that people living with impairments face different challenges when trying to assert their rights than do a number of other vulnerable groups. People with impairments are not more delicate than any other social group; rather, they are delicate in different ways.[54] People with

[54] Johan Lievens & Marie Spinoy, "*Dupin v. France*: the ECtHR going old school in its appraisal of inclusive education?", STRASBOURG OBSERVERS (Feb. 11, 2019), https://strasbourgobservers.com/2019/02/11/dupin-v-france-the-ecthr-going-old-school-in-its-appraisalof-inclusive-education/ (accessed on the 24th of July 2023).
(In this case, the European Court of Human Rights saw itself confronted with one of the key conflicts in education law: when parents and state officials disagree on which educational trajectory is best for a child with a disability, who gets the final say? This case concerned a mother fighting the decision of the French authorities to refuse her child, who has Autism Spectrum Disorder,

impairments or disabilities experience many of the same issues that children do, such as the traditional dependence on charity and paternalistic approaches. But unlike women and older people, they are a cross-class minority of the population, unlike less fortunate children. However, not everyone who has a disability experiences discrimination.

Again, at least on paper, they might be shown more leniency than other socially vulnerable groups like convicts and unauthorized immigrants, who are frequently shunned by more affluent facets of society. If people with disabilities are seen in a more sympathetic light than prisoners and illegal migrants, then it stands to reason that there will likely be a lobby group ready to demand actions to uphold their rights.

Furthermore, discrimination on the basis of disability is always viewed as unacceptable, as indirectly confirmed by the adoption and enactment of the CRPD,[55] and of the Optional Protocol (OP), which enables a single citizen of a ratifying country to directly complain to the UN CRPD Committee about his or her treatment/discrimination. While discrimination on the basis of imprisonment or on the basis of illegal immigration status is still generally permitted for instance, discrimination on the basis of disability is always regarded as unacceptable.[56] There are numerous additional ways in which people with disabilities differ considerably from people without impairments in terms of their ability to exercise their rights. First, infractions of a comparable type frequently affect people with disabilities differently from non-disabled people, especially those who have intellectual and psychosocial problems.[57] Due to their differing degree of mental development, the psychological and physical repercussions that people with intellectual disabilities feel as a result of violations of their rights and freedoms are typically greater than those faced

access to a general school (through a form of inclusive education). Instead, the child was referred to an "*Institut medico-éducatif*", an institution established to provide care and a specialized type of education to children with an intellectual impairment. Seemingly going back on its prior case law, the Court did not consider the right to education of the child to be violated.).

55 Raymond Lang. (2009). "The United Nations Convention on the right and dignities for persons with disability: A panacea for ending disability discrimination?". ALTER - European Journal of Disability Research / Revue Européenne de Recherche sur le Handicap. 3. 10.1016/j.alter.2009.04.001., p. 265.

56 Francesco Seatzu. (2020). "Empowering Persons with Disabilities: Socio-Economic Rights as a Pathway to Personal Autonomy and Independence". *Northwestern Journal of Human Rights Vol. 18*. p. 150 https://scholarlycommons.law.northwestern.edu/njihr/vol18/iss2/2 (accessed on the 5th of September 2022).

57 Monika Domańska. (2018). "People with Disabilities as a Vulnerable Group. The Concept of Protection of the Rights of Vulnerable Groups". *BIAŁOSTOCKIE STUDIA PRAWNICZE Vol. 23 Number 4*. p.28.

by people without intellectual disabilities.[58] This is certainly true with regard to the direct impact that breaches of the right to an adequate standard of living can have on an intellectually disabled person's psychological state for instance.

Think about the ability to work and find a job for instance. When their right to labour and employment is violated, PWDs are more severely impacted than non-disabled people.[59]

While it is likely that the violation of a non-disabled person's right to work will have an adverse effect on their lives, such as their ability to make a living, it is likely that the violation of a PWD's right to work and employment will have more severe repercussions.

This discrepancy takes into account the fact that employment opportunities for people with disabilities are typically lower than those for people without disabilities, which is indirectly confirmed by the data that is currently available and which demonstrates that the labor force inactivity rate of people with disabilities tends to be significantly higher than that of other workers.[60] This is also hinted at by the fact that people with disabilities are disproportionately vulnerable to the detrimental effects of unstable housing and employment conditions, as underlined by the UN Special Rapporteur on the Rights of Persons with Disabilities.[61]

Additionally, people with impairments who are members of other vulnerable groups are more likely to experience violations of their rights and freedoms than people with disabilities who do not belong to such groups.[62] All of this is dependent on how they are affected by the disadvantages and frailties brought on by their condition as disabled people as well as those brought on by incarceration, non-citizenship, position as an indigenous person, gender, etc. For instance, women with disabilities are more likely than women without disabilities to incur socio-economic rights violations, a fact that results from

---

58 Francesco Seatzu. (2020). *Loc.cit*, p. 150.

59 Marco Fasciglione. (2015). "Article 27 of the CRPD and the Right of Inclusive Employment of People with Autism". In: Della Fina, V., Cera, R. (eds*) Protecting the Rights of People with Autism in the Fields of Education and Employment*. Springer, Cham. https://doi.org/10.1007/978-3-319-13791-9_6 (accessed on the 24th of July 2023).

60 Francesco Seatzu. (2020). *Op.cit*, p. 151.

61 Ibid.

62 Neta Ziv. (2007). "The Social Rights of People with Disabilities: Reconciling Care and Justice". In D. Barak - Erez & A.M. Gross (Eds.). *Exploring Social Rights: Between Theory and Practice* (pp. 369–396). London: Hart Publishing., p. 369 at http://dx.doi.org/10.5040/9781472564214.ch-015 (accessed on the 24th of July 2023).

the specific exclusion that these women face.[63] It may be claimed that people with disabilities who experience so many disadvantages are simultaneously the targets of numerous forms of discrimination.

Finally, people with impairments are frequently potential targets of national legislation and policies that place more emphasis on rehabilitation and social security than fully distributing rights because they are founded on the premise that people with disabilities are unable to exercise the same rights as non-disabled people.[64] Systemic discrimination and structural inequality are typically to blame for violations of the rights of people with disabilities.[65] Since the repercussions of discrimination are most obviously felt in the area of socioeconomic rights, such as in the areas of employment, housing, transportation, cultural life, and access to public services, etc., this is actually not at all surprising.

Persons with impairments face many challenges in the protection of their rights. Some of these challenges include inaccessible physical environments and transportation, the unavailability of assistive devices and technologies, non-adapted means of communication, gaps in service delivery, and discriminatory prejudice and stigma in society. These challenges go a long way to prohibit an adequate enjoyment of their rights in many ways. This chapter therefore focuses on looking at the challenges that plagues the guarantee of the rights of persons with impairments (PWIs) in Cameroon.

3.1 Abuse within Institutional Settings

Abuse of persons with impairments can be identified in facilities for systematic care such as nursing homes, residential care, hospitals and day care facilities in almost every country where such institutions exist. Various people may be responsible for the abuse: a paid member of the staff, another resident, a voluntary visitor, or relatives or friends. An abusive or neglectful relationship between persons with disabilities and their caregiver at home may

---

63 Rangita de Silva de Alwis. (2009). "Mining the Intersections: Advancing the Rights of Women and Children with Disabilities Within an Interrelated Web of Human Rights". *Pacific Rim Law & Policy Journal Vol. 18 No. 1.* https://scholarship.law.upenn.edu/faculty_scholarship/1697 (accessed on the 24th of July 2023).

64 Francesco Seatzu. (2020). *Op.cit,* p. 152.

65 Steven J. Hoffman *et al.* (2016). "Is the UN Convention on the Rights of Persons with Disabilities Impacting Mental Health Laws and Policies in High-Income Countries? A Case Study of Implementation in Canada". *BMC International Health & Human Rights Vol. 16, No. 28,* at https://doi.org/10.1186/s12914-016-0103-1 (accessed on the 24th of July 2023).

not necessarily end once the person with disabilities has entered institutional care; the abuser may sometimes continue in a new setting. Though, it is often difficult to say whether the reasons for abuse or neglect found in an institutional setting have been caused by individual acts or through institutional failings, since the two are frequently found together. Abuse within the institution may take the following form;

- The provision of care for the elderly: for example, a resistance may changes in geriatric medicine, inadequate nutrition and deficient nursing care such as lack of attention towards the elderly.
- Difficulties in staff: resident interactions towards the elderly for example, poor communication, aggressiveness on the part of residents and cultural differences can result to continuous abuse of the elderly within that facility.
- The environment plays a great role in the abuse of persons with impairments within an institution. For example, a lack of basic privacy, dilapidated facilities, the use of restraints, inadequate sensory stimulation, and a proneness to accidents within the institution.[66]
- Organizational policies: the elderly persons with impairments can be abused within an institution through the operation for the benefit of the institution, giving residents few choices over daily living; bureaucratic or unsympathetic attitudes towards residents.

3.1.1 Employment and Career Challenges encountered by Persons with Impairments

Despite aspirations to be employed, many PWDs often experience challenges and barriers, including discrimination. This is frequently because of the assumed difficulties of hiring PWIs.[67] Some perceived barriers to employing PWIs include perceptions of the shortage of resources and related costs, lack of skills, and supervisors' concerns about managing PWIs.[68]

---

66 Bennett, G. et al, (1997), *The Dimensions of Elder Abuse: Perspectives for Practitioners*, London, Macmillan.

67 Lysaght R., Ouellette-Kuntz H., & Lin C.-J. (2012). "Untapped potential: Perspectives on the employment of people with intellectual disability". *Work*, *41*(4), 409–422, at https://doi.org/10.3233/wor-2012-1318 (accessed on the 13th of April 2023).

68 Kalargyrou V. (2014). "Gaining a Competitive Advantage with Disability Inclusion Initiatives". *Journal of Human Resources in Hospitality & Tourism*, *13*(2), 120–145. at https://doi.org/10.1080/15332845.2014.847300 (accessed on the 13th of April 2023).

Negative perceptions towards disabilities by both the employers and the patrons or visitors is also another challenge negatively affecting the employment of PWIs in certain sectors such as the hotel sector.[69] Accordingly, elements such as decoration, furniture, and the appearance of restaurant service personnel provide important cues for customers to make purchase decisions and evaluate service performance.[70] It is against such perceptions that the physical appearance of hotel employees comes under scrutiny by employers during the recruitment process, often placing many persons with physical disabilities at a disadvantage when employers select potential employees. The appearances and self-presentation skills of customer-facing employees therefore seem to be more important to employers in the hospitality industry than technical skills[71] to which one can arguably agree to be the case in this sector in Cameroon as we discovered in our research that many employers in this sector seek for physically attractive persons without disabilities to employ.[72] In this regard, because of discrimination, PWIs may be placed at a disadvantage during employment in the hospitality sector.

Another key challenge of employing PWIs is the provision of specialised accommodation. Employees with impairments often require specialised equipment, facility modifications, adjustments to work schedules for them to perform their professional tasks efficiently.[73] Though many employers believe in providing additional support to employees with disabilities, if required, to enhance their professional effectiveness in the place of work, the general challenge is the perceived high costs involved in providing reasonable accommodation for employees with impairments.[74] This is despite the fact that

---

69 Oliver Chikuta, Chitambara L. Rutendo & Phanos Matura. (2022). "Employment of People with Disabilities in the Hotel Sector in Zimbabwe: Challenges and Opportunities". *Review Of Disability Studies: An International Journal Vol 1 8 Issues 1 & 2,* p. 8.

70 Patterson, C. H. (2021). *Services marketing: an Asia-Pacific and Australian perspective.* Latrobe. edu.au; Frenchs Forest, N.S.W: Pearson Education Australia.

71 Nickson D., Warhurst C., & Dutton E. (2005). "The importance of attitude and appearance in the service encounter in retail and hospitality". *Managing Service Quality: AnInternational Journal, 15*(2), 195–208. At https://doi.org/10.1108/09604520510585370 (accessed on the 13th of April 2023).

72 In fact it is noticed that some employers ask as part of the documents to be submitted a full picture of the prospective applicant.

73 Sharma A., Zsarnoczky M., & Dunay A. (2019). "Development of individuals with disabilities in the hospitality sector with a focus on the importance of training and skills enhancement at all levels: A Hungarian perspective". *Littera Scripta, 12*(2). At https://doi.org/DOI.org/10.36708 (accessed on the 13th of April 2023).

74 Telwatte A. *et al* (2017). "Workplace accommodations for employees with disabilities: A multilevel model of employer decision-making". *Rehabilitation Psychology, 62*(1), 7–19. https://doi.org/10.1037/rep0000120 (accessed on the 13th of April 2023).

employers can practically convert costs incurred in training individuals with disabilities into long-term investments as it is believed that such employees are loyal and committed to their employers for a longer duration.[75]

Furthermore, the ever-changing nature of work creates significant challenges for people with impairments in finding and keeping suitable jobs. Major changes such as economic globalization, technological advancements, and population shifts are altering the nature of employment and worker skill requirements.[76] Despite rehabilitation efforts, the majority of PWDs are unemployed, though the majority of unemployed PWDs of working age desire to work. In general, PWDs vocational transition has been characterised by limited salable work skills, low income, underemployment, and unemployment.[77]

In addition, students with impairments frequently leave school without marketable skills or the capacity to function independently.[78] Given the importance of work in people's life, significantly high rates of unemployment and underemployment can harm not just the economic and social standing of persons with disabilities, but also their self-image. A particular collection of employment and career challenges faced by many people with disabilities that can be utilized as a point of reference for vocational rehabilitation and includes:

- limitations in early life experiences,
- career decision-making difficulties, and
- a negative worker self-concept

3.1.2 Limitations to Vocational Training

Frequently, people with disabilities arrive at adulthood with few career options.[79] Limited early vocational and social experiences encountered by

---

[75] Gröschl S. (2012). "Presumed Incapable". *Cornell Hospitality Quarterly*, *54*(2), 114–123. At https://doi.org/10.1177/1938965512453082 (accessed on the 13th of April 2023).

[76] Carole P. Ryan. (1995). "Work isn't what it used to be: Implications, recommendations and strategies for vocational rehabilitation". *Journal of Rehabilitation*, Vol. 61, p. 8-15.

[77] Thomas C. Curnow. (1989). "Vocational development of persons with disability". *The Career Development Quarterly, Vol. 37* No. 3, pp. 269–278. https://doi.org/10.1002/j.2161-0045.1989.tb00831.x (accessed on the 12th of April 2023.

[78] Thomas F. Harrington. (1997). *Handbook of career planning for students with special needs, 2nd ed.* PRO- ED, 8700 Shoal Creek Blvd., Austin, TX 78757-6897.

[79] Robert A. Chubon. (1985). Career- Related Needs of Schoolchildren with Severe Physical Disabilities. *Journal of Counseling & Development*, *64*(1), pp. 47-51.

people with disabilities restrict the array of career options they perceive, impede decision-making ability and impair future vocational development. The effect of limited early vocational experiences has been described as a precursor to the development of career-related problems.[80] Such problems may include failing to develop a consistent and differentiated personality pattern and a clear vocational identity and trying to make a career of a job that does not match their abilities or experiences. Unfortunately, such developmental patterns are not unusual among PWIs.

3.1.3 Segregation to Education

It is estimated that the millions of children who are out of school are relatively discriminated upon due to their sexes, cultures and because they have disabilities.[81] Thus, there will be a need for serious measures to be taken to ensure that these children who have a right to education are not left behind. The lack of adequate infrastructures, resources, finances and the recruitment of trained teachers hinders the effective guarantee of the right to education for PWIs in Cameroon.

Furthermore, though the lack of implementation of legal instruments is seen as a problem for the right of education for PWIs. Despite the fact that the government has made primary education free in government schools, it is still susceptible to certain fees such as PTA and examination fees amongst others. Unfortunately, some head teachers continue to extort money from parents and even parents with disabilities or from parents with children with disabilities. The situation is even worse with secondary schools as there has been continuous reports over the years of principals of government schools asking for bribe in order to admit students in certain schools, and those with disabilities are not left out to meet same illegal "requirement".[82] Private education is subject to high fees and though children

80 John L. Holland. (1985). *Making vocational choices: A theory of vocational personalities and work environments (2nd ed.)*. Englewood Cliffs, NJ: Prentice-Hall.

81 Mary F. Tukov. The Education of Children with Special Needs in Cameroon: The Role of Teachers and Parents towards Inclusive Education. Master Dissertation in Special Needs Education. Department of Special Needs Education, Faculty of Education, University of Oslo Norway, 2008, p. 28.

82 Government secondary and high schools such as Lycee de Dschang (Government Bilingual High School Dschang); Lycee Polyvalent de Bonaberi; Government Technical High School Bamenda (Canada); Lycee General Leclerc Yaounde and other prominent government schools, have often been reported by both media and parents for bribes in other to admit students over the years.

with disabilities or children of parents with disabilities who should benefit from tuition exemption, and other advantages, can only do so if these kids attend government schools as those in private and denominational schools are often left out from such benefits.

Furthermore, cultural hurdles to education also impede PWIs inclusion in schools. Despite the fact that some parents of PWIs want to enroll their children in school,[83] many PWIs are seen as a "disgrace" by their families, who conceal them or exclude them from contact with the rest of the community because they represent the gods' retribution on the family.[84] In this view, a PWIs is not only seen as a "bad omen that may ruin the family pedigree,"[85] but also as "unproductive and an unneeded burden," and should therefore be kept behind closed doors, away from school.[86] When these children eventually get to school, though they are sometimes accepted by some of their non-disabled peers, they are generally marginalised and despised by their teachers and fellow learners as if they are not human.[87]

3.1.4 Personal Assistance and Care Givers Challenges

Unlike high-income countries where caregivers are paid for or procured via government structures and agencies, In Cameroon, PWDs are required to pay privately for caregivers. There are very few structures and training providers such as carer agencies that provide qualified and trained substitute caregivers in general and for PWDs in particular. As a result, the vast majority of caregivers have limited or no medical or healthcare training. Even if replacement caregivers were available, they would require training, and a careful handover, which would not be possible in case a caregiver falls sick for example or has an emergency.[88]

Furthermore, for some people with mental health conditions, loneliness and social isolation from caregivers has had a significant negative impact on

83 Dan Goodley. (2011). *Disability Studies: An Interdisciplinary Introduction.* Sage publishing Ltd, London. p.138.

84 Ibid, p. 6.

85 Helene Combrinck. (2008). 'The hidden ones: Children with disabilities in Africa and the right to education" in J Sloth-Nielsen (ed) *Children rights in Africa: A legal perspective* (2008), Routledge. p. 302.

86 Djoyou S. Kamga (2013). *Op.cit.* p. 46.

87 Ibid.

88 Jalali M. *et al.* (2020). "COVID-19 and disabled people: Perspectives from Iran". *Disability Society, Vol. 35(5)*, pp. 844–847. htts://doi.org/10.1080/09687599.2020.1754165.

their emotional and psychological wellbeing. It has been reported that the potential isolation from caregivers who assist with medication adherence, together with reduced accessibility to mental health services could lead to relapse.

Furthermore, during periods of pandemics such as the COVID-19, people with impairments (and their families) carry a deep and constant fear that their caregivers may become sick and/or need to be quarantined[89] thereby leaving them alone or in the hands of strangers who may not possess adequate skills to care for them. Not only is this physically and emotionally challenging, but it also brings about additional and unbudgeted expenses. Also, some PWIs fear being admitted to hospital without their caregiver, as healthcare workers in hospitals may not have the skills, experience, training or time to provide the same necessary personal attention they need.

3.1.5 Challenges faced in Acquiring Adequate Housing

There are millions of PWIs in the world, with around 80% of them living in underdeveloped countries such as Cameroon. They generally face several barriers to exercising their right to adequate housing, including a lack of physical accessibility, ongoing discrimination and stigmatisation, institutional obstacles, a lack of labour market access, a low income, and a lack of social housing or community support. Accessibility remains a critical concern. Traditionally, homes, housing-related facilities, and neighborhoods have been intended for persons who do not have disabilities. People with disabilities are frequently excluded and marginalised, which means they are rarely addressed when new housing structures or neighborhoods are constructed, or slums are improved. They are also prone to linked rights breaches. For example, in informal communities, a lack of proper sanitation facilities might cause serious issues.

Another issue for PWIs, particularly those with intellectual or psychosocial difficulties, is legal security. Because of the frequent lack of recognition of their legal capacity, often combined with in-person application requirements, people with such disabilities are rarely able to enter into any type of formal housing contract (lease, ownership, etc.) and must rely on less

[89] Gulat G. *et al.* (2020). "People with intellectual disabilities and the COVID-19 pandemic". *Ireland Journal of Psychological Medicine, vol. 38(2)*, pp. 1–5. https:// doi.org/10.1017/ipm.2020.66 (accessed on the 31st of March 2023).

formal avenues to secure housing. As a result of these agreements, they are more subject to forcible evictions.

In general, where stigmatisation persists and social or community services, including social housing, are unavailable, persons with disabilities continue to face discrimination when seeking housing, or more general challenges in obtaining the resources required for adequate housing. Such difficulties obviously render individuals more vulnerable to eviction, homelessness, and poor living circumstances.

3.1.6 Barriers to the Provision to Health Care

Across the globe, people with impairments experience challenges in all aspects of life, including access to healthcare services, devices, required medication and support.[90] These challenges are compounded in low- and middle-income countries (LMICs) including Cameroon where factors such as poverty, poverty-related diseases, inefficient healthcare systems, training and equipment, inaccessible transportation systems, corruption, political instability, and negative attitudes towards disability occur.[91] These healthcare challenges aggravate the existing health conditions of most persons with disabilities.[92]

In times of disaster and emergencies, many people with disabilities are further marginalised and excluded, experiencing an inability to access basic health services, obtain information in an accessible format and receive therapeutic and/or medical interventions.[93] Persons with disabilities continue to experience significant barriers to accessing health care. Barriers which can be particularly severe for those residing in rural areas, can include the following:

- physically inaccessible medical clinics and hospitals;

---

90 Ashley Walker, *et al.* (2016). "When everything changes: Parent perspectives on the challenges of accessing care for a child with a disability". *Disability Health Journal* Vol. 9(1), pp. 157–161.

91 Ned Lieketseng, *et al.* (2020). "COVID-19 pandemic and disability: Essential considerations". *SAMRC Vol.* 18(2), pp. 136–148.

92 Reem Mutwali and Eleanor Ross. (2019). "Disparities in physical access and healthcare utilization among adults with and without disabilities in South Africa". *Disability Health Journal, Vol. 12(1)*, pp. 35–42 at htts://doi.org/10.1016/j.dhjo.2018.07.009 (accessed on the 31st of March 2023).

93 Emma L. McKinney, Victor McKinney, & Leslie Swartz. (2021). "Access to healthcare for people with disabilities in South Africa: Bad at any time, worse during COVID-19?" *South African Family Practice, Vol. 63(1)*, p. 1 at htts://doi.org/10.4102/safp.v63i1.5226 (accessed on the 31st of March 2023).

- lack of appropriate transport to enable them to seek medical care or rehabilitation services;
- lack of communications and accommodation in health care settings;
- untrained personnel and inadequate staffing;
- negative attitudes of health care providers;
- harmful practices, particularly in relation to persons with psychosocial disabilities;
- denial of treatment on grounds of disability, etc.

3.1.7 Lack of Adequate Means of Transport and Poor Drainage

A lack of accessible transportation is a significant barrier in accessing healthcare services, education and work for PWIs.[94] Railway networks are not accessible to wheelchair users,[95] little or no assistance is provided to assist passengers in accessing and using the different means of transportation,[96] and disabled passengers feel vulnerable because of safety concerns.[97] In addition, there are no telecoil (TTY) facilities available for passengers using hearing aids, and many transport agencies and the train stations have poor signage and unclear or no loudspeaker systems. The informal minibus taxi industry is of the main provider of public transport in Cameroon for both interurban and intraurban (especially in towns like Douala and Yaounde) transportation because of its availability and affordability. However, people with impairments experience many challenges, including lack of assistance getting into and out of a taxi, being required to lift and carry their own wheelchairs on board, being charged an extra fare for their wheelchairs and

---

[94] Sherry K. (2014). "Disability and rehabilitation: Essential considerations for equitable, accessible and poverty-reducing health care in South Africa". *South African Health Review Vol. 1*, pp. 89–99, at htt://www. hst.org.za/publications/southafrican-health-review-201415 (accessed on the 31st of March 2023).

[95] In fact most of the railways which were important in transportation of persons and goods such as the Kumba- Mbanga-Douala railway, no longer function for several reasons unknown to the public.

[96] Victor McKinney, Leslie Swartz & Emma L. McKinney, (2020). "COVID-19, disability and the context of healthcare triage in South Africa: Notes in a time of pandemic". *African Journal of Disability, Vol. 1;9(1)*, pp. 1–9. https://doi.org/10.4102/ajod.v9i0.766 (accessed on the 31st of March 2023).

[97] Grut L. *et al.* (2012). "Accessing community health services: Challenges faced by poor people with disabilities in a rural community in South Africa". *African Journal of Disability, Vol. 1(1)*, p. 19. htts://doi.org/10.4102/ajod.v1i1.19 (accessed on the 31st of March 2023).

concerns surrounding safety[98] as well as even being denied to be carried by drivers for flimsy reasons.

Furthermore, the poor nature of road network in the country is a serious hinderance to many PWIs. For those attending school or who are employed the bad state of roads seriously affect their punctuality and sometimes presence in school or at work. For those suffering from physical disabilities such as amputees and the blind, movement from and to home is often difficult. Many potholes on main roads, the lack of pedestrian paths when roads are constructed etc. Imagine the difficulty persons without disabilities go through especially during the raining season to find themselves in school or work for example, jumping one stagnant water on main roads to another or creating bush pathways in order to avoid mud or stagnant water, then one will not know how PWDs manage to step out themselves.

Also, the problem of no or poor drainage in many towns such as Douala in many neighborhoods like Bepanda, Mabanda, Bonaberi, Deido etc, which are some of the most affordable quarters were people with low income live including PWDs is a serious threat to the lives of PWIs. When it rains there is hardly any passage way in many parts or streets of these areas. Sometimes houses are overflooded as well and makes living difficult. The sanitation situation is bad and increases health problems, children in general and those with disabilities are more at risk of drowning in this overflow of water.[99] Life in general become unbearable for PWDs living in such neighborhoods as those without disability can maneuver their way out of these floods better than PWIs.

3.2 Persistent Predominance of a Discriminative Social Construct against Persons with Impairments

Discrimination underpins many Human Right violations faced by people with impairments. Despite this, age discrimination has been ignored by nearly every human right instrument to date. Disability is a social construct as much as it is a numerical category. Serotypes negative attitudes can manifest themselves through exclusion, marginalization, isolation and abuse in many forms. Structural enjoyment of equal rights is reinforced by these patterns. The

---

98 Mall S and Swartz L. (2012). "Sexuality, disability and human rights: Strengthening healthcare for disabled people". *South African Medical Journal. Vol. 102(10):* pp. 792 - 793.

99 In the month of July two children were reported dead in Bonaberi as a result of flooded water due to heavy rainfall which entered their house as the area has little or no drainage.

discrimination and maltreatment that people with disabilities face is something that affects every aspect of their lives and requires greater clarification in international and national human rights standards. Discrimination against them will be looked into from the family setting, information, health and gender. With continuous discrimination, it becomes difficult to protect persons with disabilities especially when these acts are not reported. At this point of the study, we will examine how persons with disabilities are being discriminated against at the level of their families, during armed conflicts and information and monitoring.

3.2.1 Violation of Rights during Armed Conflicts

PWDs, as individuals and as a population, have historically been subjected to egregious human rights violations on account of their impairments. These abuses include genocide, mass murder, and targeted killing; forced sterilization; involuntary medical and scientific experimentation; use of persons with disabilities as human shields, suicide bombers, and booby traps; institutionalization, sexual violence, human trafficking, and forced disappearance; and attacks against buildings dedicated to the education, health care, and rehabilitation of PWIs. Yet despite these well documented and widespread harms, PWIs, a group that comprises some one billion individuals worldwide remain largely neglected by the laws, legal processes, and institutions that seek to redress the most serious international law violations, including crimes against humanity. This is in notable contrast to the increasing prosecution of other human rights abuses as crimes against humanity such as acts of horrific violence against women and children, mass rape, and the use of child soldiers.[100]

PWIs routinely face discrimination, marginalisation and isolation in all contexts. The effects are exacerbated in situations of emergency or armed conflict, where persons with disabilities are at increased risk of acute harm, gross human rights violations, and serious violations of international humanitarian law.[101] Armed conflict has a particularly devastating and disproportionate impact on PWDs, in all phases of conflict and its consequences: for persons

[100] William I. Pons, Janet E. Lord and Michael A. Stein. (2019). "Disability, Human Rights Violations, and Crimes Against Humanity". *The American Journal of International Law, Cambridge University Press, Vol.116:1.*

[101] Francis Watene, Roberta. (2019). "Searching for the Voice of People with Disabilities in Peace and Conflict Research and Practice". *Peace & Change. 44(3)*, pp. 285-320.

in conflict zones; for those fleeing conflict; and for those in post-conflict situations or dealing with the aftermath of conflict.[102]

The devastating and disproportionate impact of conflict on PWIs has been recognised recently in the form of United Nations Security Council Resolution 2475 of June 2019.[103] Amongst other things, the Resolution stresses the disproportionate impact of armed conflict and related humanitarian crises on PWIs, and the overall responsibility of parties to armed conflict to protect civilians. It also recognises the importance of contributions by persons with disabilities to, among other things, conflict prevention, reconstruction, peacebuilding, and addressing the root causes of conflict.

During conflict, PWIs can be the subjects of targeted killings, used as human shields, and unable to access humanitarian assistance.[104] Women with disabilities are at higher risk of experiencing sexual violence. Persons with disabilities are more likely to be victims of violence or rape, and less likely to obtain police intervention, legal protection, or preventive care. In the context of fleeing conflict, refugees and internally displaced persons face exclusion from basic services.[105] Refugee and displacement camps and facilities lack formal and comprehensive procedures to identify all refugees with impairments and consequently, fail to provide them with protection and essential services, such as shelter and medical care that are accessible and responsive to their needs.[106]

3.2.2 Communication Challenges

Current healthcare policy prohibits patients from being accompanied by friends or family members when receiving healthcare, which, while a reasonable prescription in general, provides a huge barrier for a lot of persons with impairments. Many deaf people use sign language as their primary mode of communication and are unable to communicate with healthcare staff without interpreters.[107] For those who rely on lip reading, understanding healthcare

---

102 Sean Molly. (2019). 'Peace Agreements and Persons with Disabilities, Political Settlements Research Programme (PSRP)". Global Justice Academy.

103 Ibid.

104 Ibid.

105 John Twigg. (2014). "Attitude before Method: Disability in Vulnerability and Capacity Assessment" *Disasters* 38 (3): 465–482.

106 Maria Berghs. 2013. "The Global Economy of Care." In Disabling Barriers-Enabling Environments, edited by J. Swain, S. French, C. Barnes, and C. Thomas, *London: Sage*. pp. 270–276.

107 Leslie Swartz. (2014). "Five challenges for disability-related research in sub-Saharan Africa". *African Journal of Disability, vol. 3(2)*, p. 149 at htts://doi.org/10.4102/ajod.v3i2.149 (accessed on the 31st of March 2023).

workers wearing surgical masks is impossible. Furthermore, providing a patient history, or having to sign consent may be a significant obstacle, at times impossible for someone with severe intellectual or psychosocial disabilities, or on the autistic spectrum.[108]

During periods of health emergencies for example the recent COVID-19, Information about how it is transmitted and prevention measures to be taken, were released by the government across all media including television, radio and newspapers. In fact, till date a slot still runs on the national media, the Cameroon Radio Television (CRTV). However, not all of this information has been published in accessible formats, such as Braille, required by some people with disabilities. Additionally, only a few national broadcasts utilise sign language interpreters or subtitles to assist people with hearing impairments. This poses a serious challenge to their right to health.

3.2.3 Perception of Persons with Psychosocial Impairment

People who are perceived as having a psychosocial impairment or a mental health condition often face particular challenges in accessing health care and, worse, often face severe abuses in the context of care or treatment. These can include arbitrary detention in prisons or involuntary commitment to institutions, where residents may experience forced treatments and medication, verbal and physical abuse, poor conditions and overcrowding, and are often chained up for long periods of time.[109]

Abuses have also been documented at community level where, due to false perceptions about persons with psychosocial disabilities, local health care providers including traditional healers - sometimes also engage in abusive practices, often including shackling, even of children. Families and relatives are often the main support mechanisms available to individual patients with various psychosocial disabilities, but frequently struggle to provide effective support, given the lack of community-based support facilities such as out-patient medical and rehabilitation services and counselling based on free and informed consent.

---

108 Ned L. *et al.* (2020), *Op.cit*, p 137.

109 Human Rights Watch has, for example, reported on instances of shackling in countries including Ghana, Somaliland and South Sudan. available at: https://www.hrw.org/topic/disability-rights.

3.2.4 Sexual and Reproductive Health of Persons with Impairments

Reproductive health goes beyond the absence of disease or infirmity. It is a state of complete physical, mental and social wellbeing in all matters relating to the reproductive system, and at all stages of life.

Persons with disabilities have the same sexual and reproductive health needs as other persons. However, although existing services and information can usually be adapted easily to accommodate persons with disabilities, there are often barriers to accessing them. In many cases barriers are created or sustained as a result of stigma, ignorance and negative attitudes of society and individuals, including health-care providers. For example, it is often assumed that persons with disabilities are not sexually active and therefore do not need sexual and reproductive health services. In working to ensure that all sexual and reproductive health programs reach and serve persons with disabilities, increasing awareness regarding the needs and rights of persons with disabilities is critical.

The need for sexual and reproductive health services for women with disabilities is often heightened owing to their increased vulnerability to abuse. Women with disabilities experience higher rates of gender-based violence, sexual abuse, neglect, maltreatment and exploitation than women without disabilities.[110] Persons with disabilities are sometimes placed in institutions, group homes, hospitals, and other group living situations, where they may not only be prevented from making informed and independent decisions about their sexual and reproductive health, but also face an increased risk of sexual abuse and violence. Persons with intellectual and mental disabilities are particularly vulnerable in this regard. Violence against women with disabilities can also take the form of forced medical treatment or procedures, including forced sterilisation, the incidence of which has been documented in many countries and regions.

Women with disabilities have also often been denied the right to establish relationships and to decide whether, when, and with whom to have a family, in some cases being forced to marry. As a result of the increased risk of sexual violence, women with disabilities are also at risk of becoming infected with HIV and other sexually transmitted diseases. In crisis situations, these risks are multiplied.

---

110 Human Rights Watch, "Women and girls with disabilities", available at: http://hrw.org/women/disabled.html.

3.2.5 Disability Inclusion in HIV and AIDS Response

Evidence suggests that persons with disabilities are at equal, if not increased, risk of exposure to HIV. While data is scarce, a 2014 analysis of data from Sub-Saharan African countries showed that persons with disabilities are 1.3 times (1.48 for women) more at risk of contracting HIV than people without disabilities.[111] In addition, evidence suggests that persons living with HIV or those with AIDS are also at risk of developing disabilities due to illness or related treatments.[112]

Yet UNAIDS has found that persons with disabilities "represent one of the largest and most underserved populations" when it comes to health and HIV services. Barriers faced by persons with disabilities in this regard are similar to those faced in relation to access to health services generally, including lack of accessible information or education regarding HIV prevention, treatment, care and other matters and the inaccessibility of HIV testing and treatment centers due to physical barriers, poor coordination of health services and lack of accessible transport. For individuals with disabilities who are HIV-infected, poverty and barriers such as lack of transport to medical treatment centres hamper effective access to care and treatment, including antiretroviral and other medications for related infections. Persons with disabilities also experience disproportionately high levels of poverty, which further limits access to HIV prevention, treatment, care and support.[113]

3.2.6 Lack of Information

Given that access to information remains an important aspect in human life and development, people with disabilities may fail to access information and communication on health, employment, emergencies etc, as it is often not provided in accessible formats. This emerged as a serious issue in a rapid review on the impact of COVID-19 on people with disabilities.[114] Such lack of access to information on prevention and transmission, for example, could subject people with disabilities to a higher risk of contracting COVID-19. For

---

[111] UN IRIN news, Heightened HIV risk for people with disabilities, available at: http://www.irinnews.org/report/100414/heightened-hiv-risk-for-people-with-disabilities.

[112] United Nations Division for Social Policy Development, Toolkit on Disability for Africa: Inclusive Health Services for Persons with Disabilities, p. 10.

[113] *Ibid*, p. 11.

[114] Lieketseng Ned *et al.* (2020). "COVID-19 Pandemic and Disability: Essential Considerations". *Unisa Institute for Social and Health Sciences*, p. 140.

instance, people who are deaf often face challenges due to unavailability of sign language interpreters in present at offices, markets, hospitals, schools etc, and as a result of service providers not knowing or understanding sign language. Nearly all national televised broadcasts on both the CRTV and private media carry sub-titles, or sign language interpreters and so this results in many people with hearing impairments being excluded from information.[115] In addition, not being able to lip-read service providers, due to low levels of literacy among many people who are deaf, results in additional communication challenges. As such they miss various opportunities that could improve their lives or make them become aware of emergencies that they can run to safety.

3.2.7 Parental Challenges and Stigmatization

It is not uncommon to find parents with children with disabilities shielding them aware from the public or denying their disabilities. Society while growing up and even till date in many communities believe PWDs are a curse or bad omen and so they are often avoided even when they need help. It is very normal to find parents give instructions to their children not to hang around PWDs or other kids with disabilities.

Also, some parents who have children with disabilities rather than trying to integrate them within the society or try finding help for them, keep them behind locked doors for fear of stigmatisation. In fact, it may not be wrong to say that some of these parents are ashamed of their children.

Furthermore, some parents do not want to accept that their children have disabilities especially those with mental and intellectual disabilities. Such children who are meant to attend special schools are forced amongst others in normal schools and often end up not doing well. Their parents fail to take the necessary and important steps for their development and this hinders their progress.

All these stands as a serious challenge in the observance of the rights of PWDs in Cameroon as their self-development is retarded and their inclusion in society is restricted and may even cause them to become worse.

---

115 McKinney E. L., McKinney V., & Swartz L. (2020). "COVID-19, disability and the context of healthcare triage in South Africa: Notes in a time of pandemic." *African Journal of Disability, Vol. 9*, 1-9 at http://dx.doi.org/10.4102/ajod.v9i0.766 (accessed on the 16th of August 2023).

3.2.8 Gender-Bias (Women with Disabilities)

All human rights are universal and therefore unreservedly include women and men with disabilities. Every person is born equal and has the same rights to life and welfare, education and work, living independently and active participation in all aspects of society. Any direct or indirect discrimination against a PWD, be it man or woman, is a violation of his or her rights.

Women with disabilities are more vulnerable to discrimination, because they are women and because they have a disability. Many women with disabilities are further discriminated against because they are poor. This double or treble discrimination suffered by women with disabilities is often ignored or goes unnoticed because persons with disabilities are sometimes treated as though they are genderless human beings. It is also largely neglected because little information is available on its extent or impact. This situation does not appear to be improving. In 1993, for example, the then Special Rapporteur of the UN Sub Commission on Prevention of Discrimination and Protection of Minorities expressed his disappointment "at the virtually total lack of bibliographic material on the specific problems of women with disabilities."[116] Unfortunately, three decades after, there still exist the problem of limited data. The UN Standard Rules on the Equalization of Opportunities for Persons with Disabilities, adopted in December 1993, concern all people with disabilities, regardless of gender, race, age, and so forth, but contain few direct references to the gender dimension.

The 1998 report of the first General Survey on the application of ILO Convention No. 159 and Recommendation No. 168, both in States which have ratified the Convention and in those which have not, comments succinctly on equality of opportunity and treatment between disabled men and disabled women workers. People with disabilities face many obstacles in their struggle for equality. Although both men and women with disabilities are subject to discrimination, women with disabilities are double disadvantaged by discrimination based on gender and their disability status. Women with disabilities are more likely than their male counterparts to be poor or destitute, illiterate or without vocational skills, and most of them are unemployed. They have less access to rehabilitation services; they are more likely to be without

---

116 Leandro Depouy. 1993. *Human rights and Disabled Persons*. UN Center for Human Rights, New York. p.20.

family or community support and they often suffer greater social isolation due to their disability.

States parties to the UN Convention on the Elimination of All Forms of Discrimination against Women were requested to include information on women with disabilities in their periodic reports. In a sample of reports surveyed in 2001 little consistent reporting on the double discrimination experienced by women with disabilities was found.[117]

The CRPD recognizes the particular situation of women with disabilities. States Parties to the Convention undertake to recognize that "women and girls with disabilities are subject to multiple discrimination, and in this regard shall take measures to ensure the full and equal enjoyment by them of all human rights and fundamental freedoms". States Parties also undertake to "take all appropriate measures to ensure the full development, advancement and empowerment of women, for the purpose of guaranteeing them the exercise and enjoyment of the human rights and fundamental freedoms set out in the Convention."[118]

Although it might be challenging for PWDs to find employment in the open labour market, males with disabilities have nearly double the employment rate of women with disabilities. The informal sector is where most working women with disabilities can be found. Women with disabilities frequently encounter unequal hiring and promotion standards, unequal access to education and retraining, unequal access to credit and other productive resources, unequal pay for equal work, occupational segregation, and they infrequently take part in economic decision-making when they are employed.[119]

Women with disabilities are less likely to be referred to vocational training, have a harder time accessing rehabilitation programs, are less likely to obtain equality in training, and, even if they are successfully rehabilitated, are more likely to end up with part-time jobs or, worse, unemployment. This is a global trend that includes Cameroon. The perception that women with disabilities are docile, dependant, unable to perform or interested in engaging in an occupation leading to work still exists among the general public and rehabilitation counselors.

---

117 Gerard Quinn *et al.* Human rights and disability. Summary report to the Office of the UN High Commissioner on Human Rights (OHCHR), 2002.

118 Art. 6 of the CRPD.

119 International Labour Organisation. (1996). "Women swell ranks of working poor", in *World of Work* (Geneva), No. 17, Sep.-Oct. 1996 (Geneva).

According to studies, major disability assistance programs like supplemental security income, disability insurance, workers' compensation, and vocational rehabilitation disadvantage women because of their relationship to labor market participation, even in wealthy countries.[120] Not only do women receive fewer benefits than men, they also draw lower benefits. Moreover, despite their greater need, women with disabilities receive less from public income support programs.[121]

In the report of the General Survey on Convention No. 159 and Recommendation No. 168, the ILO Committee on the Application of Conventions and Recommendations states that the reports provided by governments show that the majority of nations uphold the principle of equality of opportunity in the areas of education, training, and employment, without distinction based on race, color, sex, language, or any other basis, such as disability. The general trend, however, is to create special efforts for persons with disabilities without specifically focusing on women with disabilities as a group in need of help. As a result, discrimination against women with disabilities is easily possible without being reported because the legal system is gender-neutral.

The ILO has taken a variety of actions to combat discrimination against women with disabilities in training and employment, and these actions are represented in a number of standards, resolutions, and policy statements. The ILO reiterated its concern for women employees, including those with disabilities, in the most recent resolution on ILO action for women workers, which was approved in 1991. According to ILO Convention No. 159, workers with disabilities are entitled to equal treatment and opportunity. The Convention can be utilized as part of a plan to lower obstacles that prevent women with disabilities from fully participating and being integrated into society and the economy.[122] However, one may still argue that the particular situation of women with disabilities continues to be inadequately addressed as we find them to be most of the beggars in big towns in Cameroon like Douala, Yaounde, Garoua, Maroua, or even left at home with little or no handwork to earn an income.

---

120 Arthur O"Reilly (2007). *Op.cit.* p. 49.

121 Ibid.

122 International Labour Organisation. 1998. *Vocational rehabilitation and employment of disabled persons: General survey on the Reports of the Vocational Rehabilitation and Employment (Disabled Persons) Convention (No. 159) and Recommendation (No. 168), 1983.* Report III (Part 1B) of the Committee of Experts on the Application of Conventions and Recommendations, International Labour Conference, 86th session, Geneva, 1998 (Geneva), pp. 35-36.

3.2.9 Decision-Making Ability

Lack of opportunities to participate in decision making, to form a perception of oneself as a worker and to test self-competencies can be the outcome of limited early experiences and can impede career development. The poorly defined self-concept, ambivalence about obtaining work and limited occupational information reported by people with disabilities is indicative of distortions that could result in unrealistic vocational aspirations or decisions. Many PWDs have had little opportunity for successful experience in decision making and, therefore, lack competence in making decisions.

3.2.10 Negative Worker Self-Concept

Lack of experience and difficulty in decision making are not solely the result of disability, but also an outcome of social attitudes and stereotypes. Social attitudes toward disability may be as important as the disability itself in that the negative attitude of others plays a part in shaping the life role of a PWD.[123] The outcome of this long-term exposure to prejudicial attitudes may result in a negative self-appraisal and a negative worker self- concept.

3.3 Lack of Implementation Mechanisms

At the international level, advocates for the protection of the rights of persons with disabilities argue that there are normative and implementation gaps that make the current international instruments that mentions the elderly expressly or impliedly inadequate. According to the International Human Rights Policy of 2006 a normative gap exists when a recurrent event or instrument deprives human beings of their dignity. Such a gap requires a more comprehensive instrument that can frame the rights of the affected group more clearly, even when existing instruments already provide some protection.

This has made the protection and promotion of the rights of the elderly more difficult. So many violators go unpunished because there is no standardized procedure to punish them. Member states of these conventions are reluctant to incorporate these rights in their national legislation and there

---

[123] Frank E. Fitch; (2002) "Disability and inclusion: From labeling deviance to social valuing". *Educational Theory, 52 (4)*, pp. 463-477.

is no legal repercussions for states that do not incorporated these rights in their national legislation leading to ineffective implementation.

Where laws treat individuals and groups equally, there may still be problems with implementation of those laws, that is, a *de facto* situation of inequality. When groups face particular obstacles to enjoying their rights on an equal basis with others, temporary special measures may be provided in international human rights law for the specific purpose of bringing about equality between groups. Without protection of elderly people"s human rights, any attempt for a State to remedy historical and structural violations faced by people with disabilities would leave it vulnerable to claims of discrimination by opposing groups.

As an example, Article 3 of the CEDAW states that State parties "shall take...appropriate measures" to ensure the development and advancement of women, and Article 4.1 confirms that "temporary special measures aimed at accelerating de facto equality between men and women shall not be considered discrimination". Special measures are also provided for in several articles in the CRPD, and in Articles 1.4 and 2.2 of the Convention on the Elimination of Racial Discrimination (CERD). Treaties that only implicitly include older people do not provide solid footing for State parties to address older people's rights through special measures. The UN Secretary General has remarked that the lack of special measures to ensure equality for elderly people is a major area of concern with regard to ageing.[124] In 2010, the Committee on the Elimination of Discrimination against Women drafted General Recommendation No. 27 on the gendered nature of ageing and disproportionate impact of discrimination against elderly women. Three other CEDAW Committee General Recommendations include paragraphs on particular needs and vulnerabilities of elderly women. These provide valuable insight into the CEDAW Committee's interpretation of the Convention. Without proper interpretation of the convention, implementation policy and follow up of these conventions at the national level, leaves the protection and promotion of the socio-legal rights of the elderly still remain a cause of concern.

In General Comment 6 of the Committee on Economic, Social and Cultural Rights, the Committee notes that "respect for the rights of older persons requires special measures to be taken." In addition to the somewhat

---

124 Secretary-General Report, Follow-up to the Second World Assembly on Ageing, A/66/173, July 2011.

weak language of calling for the "respect" rather than promotion, protection or advancement of human rights in instruments of human rights law, this provision is further hollowed of its weight and potential impact because it is non-binding. This is especially so when compared to ICESCR Article 10(3) which provides for special measures of protection and assistance for children and young people with respect to working conditions, and even invokes an age limit below which young people should be prohibited from working. The CRPD is insufficient to protect older people without disabilities who may seek to vindicate their right to be free from discrimination.

3.4 Conclusion

Society generally holds diminished expectations for PWIs. These attitudes are pervasive; they influence all of us to some degree. As a class, PWIs have suffered discrimination. PWIs face common social problems of stigma, marginality and discrimination, similar to those faced by members of racial and ethnic minority groups.[125]

Further, given that disability rates among racial and ethnic minority group members are proportionally higher than population overall, many individuals with disabilities face double jeopardy.[126]

Some of the difficulties faced by people with disabilities are not the result of functional impairments related to the disability, but rather are the result of classification processes embedded in societal institutions for rehabilitation and education and enforced by well- meaning professionals.[127] Classification processes have their roots in a determinist view in which people who are different are viewed as somehow less "human" or less capable.[128]

Problems of classification plague services to people with disabilities because the same categories of impairment and functional limitation (constructed mostly by people without disabilities) are used to determine

---

125 Michelle Fine & Adrienne Asch. (1988). "Disability beyond stigma: Social interaction, discrimination and activism". *Journal of Social Issues, 44*, pp. 3-21.

126 Henry T. Trueba. (1993). "Castification in multicultural America". In H. T. Trueba, C. Rodriguez, Y. Zou & J. Cintron (Eds.), *Healing multicultural America: Mexican immigrants rise to power in rural California*, Philadelphia: Falmer. pp. 29-51.

127 Edna M. Szymanski & Henry T. Trueba. (1994). "Castification of people with disabilities: Potential disempowering aspects of classification in disability services". *Journal of Rehabilitation, 60*, pp. 12-20.

128 Henry T. Trueba, Lilly Cheng & Kenji Ima. (1993). *Myth or reality : adaptive strategies of Asian Americans in California*. Washington, DC : Falmer Press.

eligibility for services, to prescribe interventions and, on occasion, to explain failure. The constructs and those who use them become agents of classification.

The disempowering nature of these classification systems is often all too apparent to people with disabilities applying for rehabilitation services in an effort to enhance self- sufficiency and personal independence.[129] Rather than being treated as adults with free or equal status, they may be confronted by persons asserting a right to determine what kinds of services they need. Thus, it is critically important that vocational rehabilitation counselors reject paternalistic classification processes and actively work to foster empowerment among consumers with disabilities during the vocational rehabilitation process. To accomplish this important task, there is the need for conceptual frameworks useful for understanding and guiding empowering vocational rehabilitation counseling approaches.

---

129 Richard K. Scotch. (2000). "Disability policy: An eclectic overview". *Journal of Disability Policy Studies, 11 (1),* pp. 6-11.

CHAPTER FOUR

A TYPOLOGY OF THE RIGHTS OF PERSONS WITH IMPAIRMENTS AS VULNERABLE GROUPS IN CAMEROON

4.0 Introduction

Persons with impairments want to be productive, but the lack of opportunities and the ensuing scarcity of resources prohibit them from doing so. This compromises their dignity and dashes whatever dreams of empowerment they may have.[130] Therefore, there is a constant need to advance knowledge of their humanity and capacities so that they are not ignored but rather given the tools they need to contribute to society in a meaningful way. They have enormous potentials that, given the right circumstances, may be unlocked and utilized for the advancement of Cameroon.

The protection and fulfilment of the rights of Persons with impairments in Cameroon is based on international, regional and national instruments, policies and principles. The presentation of these instruments take into consideration the problems of the rights of persons with impairments in different domains in the society. The international obligations on the question

[130] Lex Frieden. (2003). "Perspectives on the Status of People with Disabilities Internationally." At http://www.lexfrieden.com/_lfrieden/lfriedenperspectives0603.html (accessed on the 30th of August 2023).

of the rights of PWIs are constraining. In this sense, it gives the state the obligations to ensure the rights of PWIs are recognized. But they are also non-obligatory, that is. the state simply engages itself to ensure the respect of the rights of PWIs.

This chapter will however focus on those legal instruments that specifically deal the rights of PWIs or make mention of their rights in certain provisions as well as discuss in brief other general rights instruments due to their nature and applicability. The initiatives discuss herein are those that have been adopted as well as others that can be introduced to complement the already existing initiatives.

4.1 Rights of Persons with Impairments under International Law

This part of this work discusses, international and regional initiatives Cameroon has been party in an effort to enhance the promotion and legal protection of the rights of persons with impairments.

The UN General Assembly, at the end of 1975, proclaimed a Declaration on the Rights of Disabled Persons.[131] The Declaration affirmed that disabled persons had the same civil and political rights as other people, as well as the right to, inter alia, education, vocational training, counselling and placement services, the right to secure and retain employment or to engage in a useful, productive and remunerative occupation. The Declaration proclaimed that these rights were for all disabled persons without discrimination on the basis of sex or other grounds.

At the international level, none of the foundational human rights instruments, namely the Universal Declaration on Human Rights (UDHR), the International Covenant on Civil and Political Rights (ICCPR), or the International Covenant on Economic, Social and Cultural Rights (ICESCR) explicitly prohibits discrimination on the basis of age. To explore the exact language of those foundational documents in greater detail, the UDHR states in Article 2 that "Everyone is entitled to all the rights and freedoms set forth in this Declaration, without distinction of any kind, such as race, colour, sex, language, religion, political or other opinion, national or social origin, property, birth or other status". Our interest here is age. Although not-binding, the UDHR provides the basis, language and moral force for subsequent

131 See UN General Assembly resolution 3447 (xxx) of 9 December 1975.

human rights instruments. Both the ICCPR and the ICESCR ensure that the rights contained within are applicable to all people "without distinction of any kind, such as race, colour, sex, language, religion, political or other opinion, national or social origin, property, birth or other status". Others status here may be regarded as including age. At this level of the study, we will look at the various rights of the elderly that are spread across different conventions.

These rights will be grouped under two main categories that is, the civil and political rights of the elderly and the economic, cultural and social rights of the elderly. From a reading of the nine core international human rights treaties the International Covenant on Civil and Political Rights (ICCPR), the International Covenant on Economic, Social and Cultural Rights (ICESCR), the International Convention on the Elimination of All Forms of Racial Discrimination (CERD), the Convention on the Elimination of Discrimination against Women (CEDAW), the Convention against Torture and Other Cruel, Inhuman or Degrading Treatment or Punishment (CAT), the Convention on the Rights of the Child (CRC), the International Convention on the Protection of the Rights of all Migrant Workers and Members of their Families (ICRMW), the International Convention for the Protection of All Persons from Enforced Disappearance (CED) and the Convention on the Rights of Persons with Disabilities (CRPD) - only one prohibits discrimination on the basis of age and two mention older people.

4.1.1 Civil and Political Rights (ICCPR) of Persons with Impairments

Basic civil and political human rights have been considered of utmost importance for the protection and empowerment of older persons. These rights are generally considered to be immediately enforceable, and older persons are able to have legal claims brought on their behalf to ensure full recognition of such rights.

Persons with disabilities are considered in certain circumstances as a vulnerable group.[132] As such, state plans of action on human rights should give special attention to them and to issues of aging in general, which enhances the direct and immediate effect of civil and political

132 U.N. Human Rights Council, Report of the Special Rapporteur on Violence against Women: Its Causes and Consequences on Intersections between Culture and Violence against Women, U.N. Doc. A/HRC/4/34 (Jan. 17, 2007).

rights. Moreover, states are also required to implement positive obligations, which require programmatic measures, in order to secure adequate implementation of such rights. Civil and political rights are therefore reinforced by development cooperation, as recognized by the Economic, Social and Cultural Rights Committee in its General Comment No. 14(2000), indicating that "it is incumbent on States parties and other actors in a position to assist, to provide international assistance and cooperation, especially economic and technical, which enable developing countries to fulfil their core obligations" to this group.[133] Below are some of the civil and political rights of the elderly.

4.1.1.1 The Right to Life

According to Article 3 of the UDHR, "everyone has the right to life, liberty and security of person."[134] Every one according to this article can be interpreted to include the elderly. In the same vein, Article 6 of the ICCPR notes: "every person has the inherent right to life"... "Protected by law" and "shall not be arbitrarily deprived of life." The ICCPR does not restrict capital punishment with respect to older persons. By not limiting or restricting capital punishment for the elderly, articles 6 of the ICCPR serves or permits certain forms of violation of the rights of the elderly. It may also be that it can serve as deterrence for the elderly who are involved in grievous offences. Capital punishment is a threat and abuse to the right to life which the elderly is entitled to.

The HRC General Comment No. 6, interprets the right to life as the supreme right from which no derogation is permitted even in time of public emergency which threatens the life of the nation. However, the Committee has noted that quite often the information given concerning article 6 was limited to only one or other aspect of this right. It is a right which should not be interpreted narrowly. The Committee observes that war and other acts of mass violence continue to be a scourge of humanity and take the lives of thousands of innocent human beings every year. Under the Charter of the United Nations the threat or use of force by any State against another State, except in exercise of the inherent right of self-defense, is already prohibited. The Committee considers that States have the supreme duty to prevent wars, acts of genocide

---

133 U.N. General Assembly, Report of the Human Rights Committee-Germany, at 39 68(17), U.N.Doc. A/59/40 vol. I (2004).

134 UDHR at art. 3.

and other acts of mass violence causing arbitrary loss of life. This does not fall short of the protection of the lives of the elderly in a community. In times of war or any emergencies the state has as duty to protect the most venerable amongst whom are the elderly. Every effort they make to avert the danger of war, especially thermonuclear war, and to strengthen international peace and security would constitute the most important condition and guarantee for the safeguarding of the right to life.

The right to life means and includes all possible measures to increase life expectancy, giving older persons an enforceable right to government protection and positive measures to prolong lives. The HRC has noted that the right to life has been too often narrowly interpreted. In relation with the expression "inherent right to life," it opines that it should be interpreted broadly, and the protection of this right requires that States adopt positive measures to protect lives at all stages of the life without discrimination as to age. In another broader interpretation of the right to life, the HRC has considered that it would be desirable for state parties to take all possible measures to increase life expectancy.[135]

4.1.1.2 The Right to Recognition Before the Law

While it is important to recognize the need to protect older persons from an economic and social perspective, such efforts must be firmly grounded on the legal recognition that older persons have the inherent and inalienable right to a dignified life free from discrimination. Several human rights treaties have provisions on the right to be recognized before the law.[136] Such legal dimension includes equality under the law, equal access to justice and due process.

The issue of recognition under the law for older persons transcends national constitutional frameworks; it is reflected also in the international level where they are not specifically protected by a comprehensive thematic regime. The lack of an international convention on the human rights of the older persons also limits the legal recognition of this vulnerable group.[137] This

---

135 UN Committee on Economic, Social and Cultural Rights (CESCR), General Comment No. 14: The Right to the Highest Attainable Standard of Health (Art. 12 of the Covenant), 45, U.N. Doc. E/C.12/2000/4 (Aug. 11, 2000).

136 UDHR at art. 6; CEDAW at art. 15; CRPD at arts. 5, 12; ICCPR at art. 26.

137 Chung Working Paper, U.N. Human Rights Council, The Necessity of a Human Rights Approach and Effective United Nations Mechanism for the Human Rights of the Older Person, 58, A/HRC/AC/4/CRP.1 (2010).

situation simply compounds their vulnerable situation at both national and international levels.[138]

The difference between *de jure* and *de facto* status of State obligations to elderly persons is sometimes very great. Where states include national legal recognition of the rights of elderly persons, such recognition is not always upheld and may even be undermined by unacceptable national practices. A lack of identification is just one of the barriers that may prevent older persons from fully realizing their rights. Such situations can severely limit the exercise of many other rights by older persons, including autonomy and self-determination, and access to legal services as well as to health and other social services.

The general scope of the right to legal recognition is set out in Article 6 of the UDHR and Article 16 of ICCPR which state that everyone has the right to recognition everywhere as a person before the law. However, international human rights law lacks an explicit definition of the legal status of older persons that would reflect their particularly vulnerable position. Where older people's specific situations are not expressly referenced and their specific rights, needs and challenges are not well articulated, older people face rights violations that deprive them of dignity, integrity of person, security of person and even life, without any recourse to justice or redress. The consequence of excluding age from explicit prohibited grounds for discrimination is that States are not prompted to report on the situation of older people. They are therefore less likely to ensure older people are included within national law, programs or initiatives, or to ensure equality across groups.

4.1.1.3 The Right to Freedom from Violence

Several human rights treaties recognize the human rights to life, liberty, and security of person.[139] In this legal framework, persons with disabilities have the right to be free from all forms of abuse (physical, emotional, or financial, among others), as well as the right to enjoy the state's protection from all forms of exploitation and marginalization. Abuse of older persons can take the form of physical abuse, which refers to the infliction of physical or psychological harm or injury, or sexual abuse, in every country and every

138 Bonn Germany Expert Group Meeting on the Rights of Older Persons, May 5–7, 2009 pg 15.

139 UDHR, Art. 3 Convention on the Rights of the Child (CRC), Art. 2; CRPD, Art. 16.

economic income bracket.[140] The United Nations General Assembly on the follow-up of the Second World Assembly on Ageing stressed that "Older women tend to be at most risk, as they live longer than men do and culturally are often more vulnerable to abuse."[141]

The Toronto Declaration on the Global Prevention of Elder Abuse defines "elder abuse" as "a single or repeated act, or lack of appropriate action, occurring within any relationship where there is an expectation of trust, which causes harm or distress to an older person."[142] The UN High Commissioner for Human Rights in the report submitted before the UN during the first months of 2012 determined that "the abuse of older persons may be physical, psychological, sexual and emotional."[143]

Abuse committed against older persons is one of the most prevalent forms of abuse. Elder abuse is a single or repeated act or lack of appropriate action occurring within any relationship where there is an expectation of trust, which causes harm or distress to an older person.[144] Abuse, however, is not the only type of violence older persons face. Many older men and women, especially older women, experience violence in their homes, in care settings, or in conflict or post-conflict situations.[145]

Harmful practices targeted specifically at older women and men, including violence because of superstition or witchcraft accusations and elder abuse, have not been adequately addressed.[146] The victims of accusations of witchcraft who suffer the most serious violence are invariably older women. The international community should highlight the abuse of older women, and they should receive targeted funding.[147] Concern about persecution of persons

140 U.N. Human Rights Council, Agenda and Annual Programme of Work, 11, U.N. Doc. A/HRC/4/121 (June 18, 2007).

141 U.N. Secretary-General, U.N. Department of Economic and Social Affairs Division for Social Policy and Development Programme on Ageing: Report of the Expert Group Meeting Rights of Older Persons, 34 (2009).

142 World Health Organization, *The Toronto Declaration on the Global Prevention of Elder Abuse*, 32 (2002), http://www.who.int/ageing/projects/elder_abuse/alc_toronto_declaration_en.pdf. Bolima S. Ambang, Socio-Legal Protection of the Vulnerable Group under International Law: Case Study of the Elderly, PhD Thesis, University of Soa, Faculty of Law and Political Science, (Unpublished).

143 U.N. Economic and Social Council, Substantive Session of 2012: Report of the High Commissioner for Human Rights, U.N. Doc. E/2012/51 (Apr. 20, 2012).

144 World Health Organization, *The Toronto Declaration on the Global Prevention of Elder Abuse*, 32 (2002), http://www.who.int/ageing/projects/elder_abuse/alc_toronto_declaration_en.pdf.

145 HelpAge Position Paper .Climate change in an ageing world Originally published 9 Dec 2015.

146 HelpAge International, *supra*.

147 U.N. Office of the High Commissioner for Human Rights, Report of the Special Rapporteur on violence against women, its causes and consequences, Mission to Ghana U.N. Doc. A/HRC/7/6/

accused of witchcraft practices has long been recognized as a major issue in sub-Saharan Africa. In Nigeria, the persecution of elderly women suspected to be witches is predominantly widespread, and has been identified as one of the most important obstacles to the attainment of the December, 1993 Declaration of the UN General Assembly on elimination of violence against women on the continent. Torturing and various forms of violence against elderly women accused of witchcraft without evidence against them implies major infringements of their fundamental Human Rights as enshrined in Article 5 of the Universal Declaration of Human Rights which stipulates that no one shall be subjected to torture or to cruel, inhuman, or degrading treatment or punishment. Despite this and other similar instruments, persecution of elderly women suspected of witchcraft remains unabated in Nigeria.[148] Furthermore, there is little scholarly work and insufficient government policies in Nigeria to address this issue. This is an attempt to bridge this gap.

The 2012 report of the UN High Commissioner for Human Rights pointed out that "the consequences of physical violence for elderly persons can be serious and they are more likely to require longer periods of recuperation even from minor Injuries. Apart from causing severe and lasting emotional distress, physical violence is also a cause of premature mortality among older persons."[149] Violence can cause irreparable harm.

In violent conflicts, elderly persons make up a disproportionate percentage of civilian casualties[150]. It is the recommendation of a group of special rapporteurs that the HR Council reiterate calls to end violence against civilians including elderly persons in conflict areas.[151]

Add.3, at no. 65 and conclusion (Feb. 21, 2008); U.N. Human Rights Council, Report of the Special Rapporteur on Violence Against Women: Its Causes and Consequences ,at no.123, U.N. Doc. A/HRC/11/6/Add.5 (May 27, 2009); Human Rights Council, Report of the Special Rapporteur on Extrajudicial, Summary or Arbitrary Executions, Philip Alston: Addendum: Mission to the Central African Republic, at no. 49,, U.N. Doc. A/HRC/11/2/Add.3.

148 Eboiyehi, F.A. (2017), "Convicted without evidence: Elderly women and witchcraft accusations in contemporary Nigeria", *Journal of International Women's Studies*, volume 18, pages, 247-265.

149 U.N. Economic and Social Council, *Substantive Session of 2012: Report of the High Commissioner for Human Rights*, 33, U.N. Doc. E/2012/51 (Apr. 20, 2012) http://www.un.org/ga/search/view_doc.asp?symbol=E/2012/51.

150 U.N. Human Rights Council, Report of the Independent Expert Appointed by the Secretary General on the Situation of Human Rights in Somalia (Mr GhanimAlnajjar), 18, U.N. Doc.A/HRC/7/26 (Mar. 17, 2008).

151 U.N. Human Rights Council, Updated report on the situation of human rights in Darfur prepared by the United Nations Experts Group on Darfur, presided by the Special Rapporteur on the situation of human rights in Sudan and composed by the Special Representative of the Secretary General for children and armed conflict, the Special Rapporteur on extrajudicial, summary on arbitrary executions, the Special Representative of the Secretary-General on the human rights

One Special Rapporteur points out that in a conflict where half of all civilian casualties are children and older persons, the argument is strengthened that an occupying military operation, by its intrinsic nature, generates war crimes.[152]

4.1.1.4 The Right to Equality and Non-Discrimination

Every human has inalienable rights regardless of their age.[153] However, the non- discrimination clauses in international law rarely specify age as a prohibited ground for discrimination. While human rights law prohibits discrimination on several grounds, age could be argued to be included in the phrase "and other status." Some of this is a result of ageism. One definition of ageism is a systematic stereotyping and discrimination against persons because they are old. Sometimes ageism is compared to sexism or racism because it discriminates against all members of a particular group. The principles of equality and non-discrimination require taking special measures to protect segments of society with a history of discrimination as a matter of priority.[154] Clearly, as it was highlighted in the of Report of the Expert Group Meeting on the "Rights of Older Persons" discrimination, neglect and abuse are in daily feature in the lives of many older persons.

The right to equality before the law and the principle of non-discrimination are universal human rights foundations enshrined in Articles 1 and 2 of the UDHR which provides that all human beings are "born equal in dignity and rights" and "everyone is entitled to the same rights and freedoms without distinction of any kind", including distinctions based on "other status." "Other

defenders, the Representative of the Secretary-General on human rights internally displaced persons, the Special Rapporteur on the question of torture and the Special Rapporteur on violence against women: its causes and consequences, U.N. Doc. A/HRC/6/7 (Sept. 22, 2007).

152 U.N. General Assembly, *Report of the Special Rapporteur on the Situation of human rights in the Palestinian territories occupied since 1967: note/by the Secretary-General*, at no. 23, U.N.Doc. A/HRC/10/20 (Feb. 11, 2009).

153 Universal Declaration of Human Rights (UDHR), Article 2; Convention on the Rights of Persons with Disabilities (CRPD), Article 5; International Covenant on Civil and Political Rights(I CCPR), Article 2.

154 U.N Human Rights Council, Report of Independent Expert on human rights and extreme poverty, Rapporteur:. "To collect information to prepare this report the independent expert sent a questionnaire to Governments requesting information on their social pensions for older persons. The questionnaire addressed: (i) the legal and institutional framework; (ii) the schemes costs and coverage; (iii) implementation procedures; (iv) monitoring mechanisms and complaints procedures; and (v) studies and evaluations", 58 (Magdalena Sepulveda 2010)(hereinafter "Sepulveda Report").

Status" here can be interpreted as including the elderly. Article 26 of ICCPR further links these two principles, stating that "all persons are equal before the law and are entitled without any discrimination to the equal protection of the law. In this respect, the law shall prohibit any discrimination and guarantee to all persons equal and effective protection against discrimination on any ground." Theoretically, this should include the elderly that fall under the "other status" of Article 1 of the UDHR.

The ICCPR states that distinctions of "other status," such as age, are outlawed. It further requires in its Article 2 that the state parties "respect and ensure the rights recognized therein to all individuals within their jurisdiction"[155]. The elderly are a vulnerable group within any state and their protection should not be over looked. The ICCPR also provides a list non-derogable rights even in times of public emergency, which is of particular relevance to elderly persons, who are often more vulnerable in such situations. In Article 4, it provides that even "in time of public emergency which threatens the life of the nation and the existence of which is officially proclaimed, the state parties may take measures derogating from their obligations under the ICCPR to the extent strictly required by the exigencies of the situation" and they cannot "involve discrimination solely on the ground of race, colour, sex, language, religion or social origin."[156] Where older people's specific situations are not expressly referenced and their specific rights, needs and challenges are not well articulated, the elderly are bound to face older violations that deprive them of dignity, integrity of person, security of person and even life, without any recourse to justice or redress.

This group-based or "vulnerable group" approach is applicable in the context of civil and political, as well as economic, social, and cultural rights. Culture and tradition may influence the extents to which elderly persons are discriminated against in daily life. Direct age discrimination could involve less favourable treatment because of a person's actual age, such as not hiring someone because you decide they are too young to be competent in a job role or from your perception about a person's age, you treat someone less than you treat others. The third type is associative age discrimination. This is when you treat someone less favourably due to someone else's age. This person could be a friend, spouse, partner, or anyone they associate with. Equal treatment is important for all people.[157] In relation to government programs, elderly persons

155 ICCPR, Art. 1.

156 ICCPR, No derogation from articles 6, 7, 8 (paragraphs I and 2), 11, 15, 16 and 18.

157 UN Human Rights Council, Report of the Special Rapporteur on Contemporary Forms of

are often "denied equity in opportunities available to them and in resources allocated to them."[158] Additionally, the HRC states in its General Comment No. 18 that the grounds for discrimination are not limited to those expressly mentioned in the ICCPR.[159] In litigation of the right to non-discrimination, the HRC has applied the right to equal protection under Article 26 of the ICCPR to economic, social and cultural rights. It is demonstrated that certain economic, social and cultural rights are judicially enforceable through the right to equality and non-discrimination. One method to achieve this would be an appeal based on Article 26 ICCPR. The Human Rights Committee has pointed out that the non-discrimination clause of Article 26 ICCPR has an independent nature and is not limited to those rights that are provided for in the ICCPR. It can be invoked regarding rights not set out in the ICCPR and may therefore provide protection against discrimination in the enjoyment of economic, social and cultural rights.

4.1.1.5 The Right to Freedom from Cruel, Inhuman or Degrading Treatment or Punishment

According to Article 5 of the UDHR "no one shall be subjected to torture or to cruel, inhuman or degrading treatment or punishment." Similarly, according to Article 7 of the ICCPR, "no one shall be subjected to torture or to cruel, inhuman or degrading treatment or punishment," including, "without his free consent, to medical or scientific experimentation." In General Comment No. 20 on Article 7 about the prohibition of torture, or other cruel, inhuman or degrading treatment or punishment, the Human Rights Committee stated that "special protection in regard to experiments is necessary in the case of persons not capable of giving their consent." "More attention should be given to the possible need and means to ensure the observance of this provision."[160] All these provisions do not specifically meet the needs the elderly. The situations are not expressly referenced on their specific rights, reasons for the violations of their socio-legal rights.

Racism, Racial Discrimination, Xenophobia and Related Intolerance, DoudouDiène: addendum: mission to Lithuania,, U.N. Doc. A/HRC/7/19/Add.4 (Feb. 7, 2008).

158 Committee on Economic, Social and Cultural Rights, General comment No. 6: The economic, social and cultural rights of older persons, U.N. Doc. E/1996/22 (1996).

159 UN Human Rights Committee (HRC), CCPR General Comment No. 18: Non-discrimination.

160 Torture or Cruel, Inhuman or Degrading Treatment or Punishment: General Comment 7, U.N.GAOR, H um. Rts. Comm., 16th Sess., 7, U.N. Doc. HRI/GEN/1/Rev.1 (1994).

As concerns what would amount to torture against the elderly, the Second Working Session of the UN Open-Ended Working Group on Ageing held on August 2011, the Chair of the United Nations Committee against Torture emphasized that "the definition of torture takes into account the particular circumstances of an individual, including their health conditions and age. It is the duty of States to investigate and punish any conduct that can amount to inhuman or degrading treatment, in places like psychiatric institutions or prisons where older persons may not be able to take action to protect themselves."[161]

The right to be free from torture enjoys in-depth protection thanks to the Convention against Torture and Other Cruel, Inhuman or Degrading Treatment or Punishment ("CAT"),[162] which is entirely dedicated to the topic. The CAT defines torture within the framework of the instrument as: "any act by which severe pain or suffering, whether physical or mental, is intentionally inflicted on a person, or for any reason based on discrimination of any kind, when such pain or suffering is inflicted by or at the instigation of or with the consent or acquiescence of a public official or other person acting in an official capacity."[163] Although this provision does not mention the elderly, the elderly do suffer discrimination from the society due to their age. This has caused the elderly to live a solitary life of pain in their homes. It will be salutary for member States to incorporate this provision in their national laws to protect the elderly from societal discrimination.

Likewise, Article 10 establishes the state's duty to "ensure that education and information regarding the prohibition against torture are fully included in the training of law enforcement personnel, civil or military, medical personnel, public officials and other persons who may be involved in the custody, interrogation or treatment of any individual subjected to any form of arrest, detention or imprisonment."[164] Article 16 further expands the scope by obliging state parties to "undertake to prevent in any territory under its jurisdiction other acts of cruel, inhuman or degrading treatment

161 Report of the Open-ended Working Group on Ageing for the Purpose of Strengthening the Protection of the Human Rights of Older Persons, G.A. Res. 65/182, U.N. Doc. A/Res/65/182(Aug. 4, 2011).

162 ICCPR, Art. 7 (commenting that individuals should not be subjected to torture or cruel punishment and stating that people should not be forced to participate in medical or scientific experiments without their consent).

163 Convention against Torture and Other Cruel, Inhuman or Degrading Treatment or Punishment, G.A. Res. 39/46, art. 1, U.N. Doc. A/39/51 (June 26, 1987), hereinafter UNCAT.

164 Ibid, Art. 10.

or punishment which do not amount to torture as define in Article 1." This may be particularly relevant for older persons in situations of vulnerability to inhuman or degrading treatment by non-state actors. Where the state has reason to know of the treatment, it has a duty to implement actions to prevent it. Its treaty body, the Committee Against Torture ("CAT Committee"), refines the meaning of the provisions through its general comments and individual complaint mechanism.

As the people grow old in age, they tend to be more dependent on their children and others. Many elderly persons become increasingly vulnerable to abuse and exploitation in residential care facilities and in families. The HRC, for example, noted the vulnerable situation of elderly persons placed in long-term care homes, which in some instances has resulted in degrading treatment and violated their socio-legal rights and their human dignity within the society. States are being encouraged to double their efforts to improve the situation of elderly persons in nursing homes and the society at large.[165] The CAT also sets basic procedural standards in its Article 13 when it calls upon state parties to "ensure that any individual who alleges he has been subjected to torture in any territory under its jurisdiction has the right to complain to, and to have his case promptly and impartially examined by, its competent authorities."

4.1.1.6 The Right to Liberty and Security

Along with the right to life, the right to liberty is one of the most fundamental human rights. The right to liberty is the right of all persons to freedom of movement and freedom from arbitrary detention by others. No one shall be subjected to arbitrary arrest or detention. Alongside the right to liberty we have the right to security which means States are required to take reasonable measures to protect a person's security (both physical and mental). The government does this through the work of the police and emergency services, for example. Article 9 of the International Covenant on Civil and Political Rights (ICCPR) subsection 2 states that, a person must not be subject to arbitrary arrest or detention. This brings us to the socio-legal rights of the elderly. States are required to protect the elderly at all cost within their jurisdiction in accordance with their right to liberty and security.

165 U.N. Human Rights Committee, General Comment No. 6: The Right to Life, U.N. Doc.HRI/GEN/1/Rev.9 (Vol. I) (Apr. 30, 1982).

Pursuant to Article 9 of the ICCPR, everyone has the right to liberty and security; "no one shall be deprived of his liberty except on such grounds and in accordance with such procedure as are established by law", and arbitrary arrest or detention is prohibited. It is prohibited to arbitrarily discriminate against an elderly and detain the elderly. The ICCPR in Article 10 establishes that "persons deprived of their liberty should be treated with humanity and with respect for the inherent dignity of the human person." For older persons, this is an important protection for those in state and private long-term care facilities, and living with other forms of institutionalization for their protection. If this provision is fully implemented by that states, the elderly will enjoy some degree of protection and respect of their human rights. One's liberty is directly affected by legal capacity, defined as "the right to access the civil and juridical system and the legal independence to speak on one's own behalf."[166] The Convention on the Rights of Persons with Disabilities in Article 12(2) ("CRPD") outlines that the right to make choices freely is not contingent on legal capacity; it influences how much support is needed to exercise one's rights. The ICCPR supports the view by providing that everyone lawfully within the territory of a state shall, within that territory, have the right to liberty of movement and freedom to choose his residence.[167] A further right related to the protection of liberty and security is the right to fair trial as enshrined in Article 11 of the UDHR. This requires procedural due process for restrictions of liberty in advance of a criminal trial, regardless of age or other status.

4.1.1.7 The Right to Respect for Home and Family

People with disabilities need to be respected and it is one way of making them feel special. This is noticeable when their faces brighten up and their morale boosts up, when we respect them, listen to them, and express our love and kindness towards them, show respect towards the elderly, spend time with them, be polite, ask for advice, eat together, discuss family heritage, history and traditions, call them and tell them how much we appreciate and respect them. Family provides care to elderly people. Family provides different forms of care and support including advocacy. These are especially important

166 Explanatory Note on Legal Capacity and Forced Interventions, international Disability Caucus, Explanatory Note on Legal Capacity and Forced Interventions (2014).

167 Article 12 of the ICCPR.

for older adult with mental health history, disabilities and those residing in nursing home. Family support influences the care individuals receive when living in nursing homes.

General human rights law includes a number of provisions for the environment of the home and family. Article 23 of the ICCPR establishes that the family is the natural and fundamental group unit of society and is entitled to protection, including that the right of men and women of marriageable age to marry and to found a family shall be recognized. To make this effective, States are expected to take appropriate steps to ensure equality of rights and responsibilities of spouses as to marriage, during marriage and at its dissolution.[168]

Article 10 of the ICESCR recognizing the right to respect for home and family provides that States are to take appropriate measures to ensure equality of rights and responsibilities of spouses as to marriage regardless of age during marriage and at its dissolution. The CESCR encourages states to support, protect, and strengthen the family because many cultures believe that the family unit must provide care for older persons.[169] It also suggests that those elderly persons who prefer to stay at home should not be discriminated against, and should be provided for through services from both government and non-governmental agencies.

The CESCR further suggests that states provide financial support to family members caring for older persons at home, particularly poor families. States should also provide financial and logistical assistance to older persons living alone and to elderly couples who prefer to stay in their own home. The assistances should include transportation, food delivery, nursing care, and doctors visits. In sum, the state should encourage the cultural decision to keep the family unit together. Resources that might be spent building nursing homes should instead be spent on compensating families for caring for their elderly relatives at home.

---

168 Article 23 of ICCPR.

169 General Comment 6, para. 31 (stating that Recommendation 29 encourages governments and non- governmental organizations to implement social service programs to support the whole family). U.N. Human Rights Committee, General Comment No. 6: The Right to Life, 31, U.N. Doc. HRI/GEN/1/Rev.9 (Vol. I) (Apr. 30, 1982)(stating that Recommendation 29 encourages governments and non-governmental organizations to implement social service programs to support the whole family.

4.1.1.8 The Right to Information, Association and Participation

The Right to Information empowers every citizen to seek any information from the Government, inspect any Government documents and seek certified photocopies thereof. Right to Information also empowers citizens to officially inspect any Government work or to take the sample of material used in any work. The principle of public participation holds that those who are affected by a decision have a right to be involved in the decision-making process. Public participation implies that the public's contribution will influence the decision.

Many international human rights instruments embody the guarantee to information, association and participation by preserving rights to expression, association and participation in cultural life.[170] The scope and status of the right is also outlined in general terms in the primary instruments of the International Bill of Rights. Article 27 of the UDHR elaborates that "everyone has the right freely to participate in the cultural life of the community, to enjoy the arts and to share in scientific advancement and its benefits" as found in ICESCR Article 15. The elderly are often considered as not having a place in the society especially those elderly citizens that are found in developing countries and are in the rural communities. This group of people are often marginalized and discriminated upon; as such, they find it difficult to fully participate in public due to fear of abuse from the community. The International Bill of Rights includes a number of provisions that establish the rights to association and participation. The elderly have the right to create an association that they can freely elaborate on matters that concerns them without any restriction. Article 20 of the UDHR guarantees the right of everyone to freedom of peaceful assembly and association. Furthermore, Article 21 of the ICCPR states that "no restrictions may be placed on the exercise of this right other than those imposed in conformity with the law."

Article 25 of the ICCPR codifies the right to participate in public affairs. This article was further elaborated by the Human Rights Committee in General Comment 25, where they took a broad interpretation of the right to participate in public affairs, to include the right of all citizens especially the elderly to participate directly by voting in referenda, by being elected, or presumably by participating in other means of direct democracy. Also, the

---

170 Article 15 of the ICESCR.

elderly can freely choose their representatives that are elected according to international election obligations and standards. The elderly can participate in consultative processes, debate and dialogue when called upon without any discrimination. The elderly can establish and join organizations that will positively affect them including civil society organizations, unions and political parties. Equal access to public service positions should not be something just for the younger population but for the elderly as well including employment in public. Additionally, Article 8 of the ICESCR establishes the right to labour organization without state interference as the "state parties undertake to ensure the right of everyone to form trade unions and join the trade union of his choice, subject only to the rules of the organization concerned, for the promotion and protection of his economic and social interests." So far, no such organization of labour has taken up the issue of the human rights of its aging members.

Furthermore, Article 25 of the ICCPR stipulates that "every citizen shall have the right and the opportunity, without any of the distinctions mentioned in Article2 and without unreasonable restrictions: to take part in the conduct of public affairs either directly or through freely chosen representatives." General Comment No. 25 supports the principle that each person's vote should be equal to each other person's vote.[171] An older person's vote should in no way be diminished from a younger person's vote.

Exclusion can be exacerbated by physical barriers to participation. Article 2 of the CRPD defines, *inter alia*, "universal design" as "the design of products, environments, programs and services to be usable by all people, to the greatest extent create sanitation facilities designed to facilitate access to water and sanitation for everyone, possible, without the need for adaptation or specialized design."[172] States must create sanitation facilities designed to facilitate access to water and sanitation for everyone.

171 Human Rights Committee, General Comment 25 UN Human Rights Committee (HRC), CCPR General Comment No. 25: Article 25 (Participation in Public Affairs and the Right to Vote), The Right to Participate in Public Affairs, Voting Rights and the Right of Equal Access to Public Service, CCPR/C/21/Rev.1/Add.7, (July 12 1996).

172 General Assembly resolution 61/106, annex I. UN General Assembly, Convention on the Rights of Persons with Disabilities: resolution/ adopted by the General Assembly, A/RES/ 61/106, (Jan. 24 2007) available at http://www.refworld.org/docid/45f973632.html. Convention on the Rights of Persons with Disabilities, 2515 U.N.T.S. 3. (May 3, 2008).

4.1.2 Economic Social and Cultural Rights of Persons with Impairments

The Committee on Economic, Social and Cultural Rights (CESCR) is the body of 18 independent experts that monitors implementation of the International Covenant on Economic, Social and Cultural Rights by its States parties. The Committee was established under ECOSOC Resolution 1985/17 of 28 May 1985 to carry out the monitoring functions assigned to the United Nations Economic and Social Council (ECOSOC) in Part IV of the Covenant. The International Network for Economic, Social and Cultural Rights is a collaborative initiative of groups and individuals from around the world working to secure economic and social justice through human rights. As there is no complaint procedure under the ICESCR, the primary mechanism for its enforcement is the state reporting process. Specialized agencies provide information relevant to the report being considered. Committee members then put questions and observations to the State party and responses are provided. The ICESCR falls under the third generation of human rights since it deals with hose rights which include right to self-determination, economic and social development, healthy environment, natural resources, and participation in cultural heritage.[173]

4.1.2.1 The Right to an Adequate Standard of Living

Older persons are a particularly vulnerable group that is specially exposed to poverty and its consequences. Even in the wealthiest countries on earth that pride themselves on social protection in old age, older women have a poverty risk rate of about 22% and older men have a poverty risk rate of 16%.[174] Precise information about poverty in old age is difficult to ascertain. As the Independent Expert on Human Rights in Extreme Poverty has suggested, "weaker knowledge of the specificities of old-age poverty most likely leads to policy choices that ignore and possibly exclude older persons living in extreme poverty."[175]

---

173 Karel, V. (2019), *Generations of Rights and the Contemporary Human Rights Discourse*, Springer Nature Switzerland AG.

174 UN Committee on Economic, Social and Cultural Rights (CESCR), General Comment No. 6: The Economic, Social and Cultural Rights of Older Persons, 13, U.N. Doc. E/1996/22 (Dec. 8, 1995).

175 Ibid. Pg 7.

The CESCR linked this right to the inherent dignity of all persons and marked its indispensability to the fulfillment of virtually every other right in the International Bill of Rights, including the ICCPR and ICESCR, among others.[176] Moreover, it has attached great importance to the right to an adequate standard of living, as it includes the right to "adequate food, water, shelter, clothing and healthcare through the provisions of income, family and community support and self-help." In addition, Article 25 of the UDHR sets the standard that requires states to ensure the "right to security in the event of unemployment, sickness, disability, widowhood, old age or other lack of livelihood in circumstances beyond his control." In this light, if article 25 of the UDHR is fully implemented, the socio-legal rights of the elderly will be protected. States that have ratified and incorporated this article into their national laws, implementation and follow up has to be improved upon to fully guarantee the socio-legal of the elderly.

An adequate standard of living encompasses many different aspects of life. As already mentioned, the CESCR has interpreted this to include several social and economic rights.[177] Article 10 of the ICESCR requires states to accord "the widest possible protection and assistance to the family, which is the natural and fundamental group unit society."[178] As Lindsay Judge puts it CESCR General Comment No. 6 also points to the need to support families in responding to the needs of older relatives. Specifically, it stresses the need for measures to support low-income families in caring for older persons as well as single persons or elderly couples who wish to remain in their homes.

4.1.2.2 The Right to Food to under ICESCR

With regard to the General Comment No. 12 on the right to food, issued by the Committee of the ICESCR, the human right to adequate food is of fundamental importance for the enjoyment of all rights, as the right to adequate food is indivisibly linked to the inherent dignity of the human person and is essential for the implementation of other human rights, such

176 U.N. Committee on Economic, Social and Cultural Rights (CESCR), General Comment No. 6: The Economic, Social and Cultural Rights of Older Persons, 32, U.N. Doc. E/1996/22 (Dec.8, 1995)(describing how the right to adequate food is linked to human dignity and social justice).

177 Rodriguez-Pinzon, D and Claudia, M. (2003), "The International Human Rights Status of Elderly Persons", *American University International Law Review*, Volume 18, issue 4, page, 960.

178 Lindsey Judge, The Rights of Older People: International Law, Human Rights Mechanism and the Case for New Normative Standards 7 (2009).

as the right to life.[179] The comment underlines that the right to adequate food "means physical and economic access at all times to adequate food or means for its procurement."[180] This is a right recognized by many states as a fundamental right. A state's economic vulnerability and widespread poverty affects vulnerable groups, including elderly persons, who can be prone to food insecurity.

The CESCR interprets the scope of the right to adequate food in General Comment No 12, stating that pursuant to Article 11 of the ICESCR, states recognize the right of everyone to an adequate standard of living for himself and his family, including adequate food, clothing and housing, and to the continuous improvement of living conditions, which necessarily implies the right of everyone to be free from hunger. The core aspects of the right to adequate food include "the availability of food in a quantity and quality sufficient to satisfy the dietary needs of individuals, free from adverse substances, and acceptable within a given culture. This includes the accessibility of such food in ways that are sustainable and that do not interfere with the enjoyment of other human rights. States that are signatories to this convention have as objective to implement this right as far as the elderly are concerned within their jurisdiction. The socio-legal rights of the elderly can only be protected with the full collaboration of the government. Without this, the elderly are left to be violated one way or the other in the society.

4.1.2.3 The Right to Education and Culture

The right to education is essential to ensure the fulfillment of the civil, political, economic, social and cultural rights.[181] This right clearly articulates the notions of indivisibility and interdependence of all human rights.[182] Older persons generally experience severe limitations in the enjoyment of the right to education, including access to literacy training as well as other holistic educational activities (cultural, spiritual, recreational, etc.),[183] due to the social preconception that education is to be delivered to younger

---

179 General Comment 12 Right to Adequate Food, U.N. Doc. E/C.12/1999/5 CESCR, 20th Sess. 4, (1999).

180 Ibid article 14.

181 Manfred, N. (1995), *The Right to Education, in Economic, Social and Cultural Rights: A Textbook*, BemanAssociate 4611-F Assembly Drive.

182 Plans of Action for Primary Education (Art. 14): General Comment 11, U.N. Econ., Soc., & Cultural Rights. Comm., 20th Sess., 2, UN Doc. E/C.12/1999/4 (1999).

183 CRC, Article 28; CRPD, Article 24; ICESCR, Article 13.

generations. A non-discrimination approach on the right to education is stipulated in Article 26 of UDHR, which states that technical and professional education shall be made generally available and higher education shall be equally accessible to all on the basis of merit. Further, Article 26 elaborates on the scope of the right stating that "education shall be directed to the full development of the human personality and to the strengthening of respect for human rights and fundamental freedoms." Age should not be a discriminating factor for the elderly to pursue their educational goal, often time the elderly are being mocked when they decide the take up studies at a later stage in their lives. This provision should be well implemented within the society.

The right to education includes a variety of dimensions, such as access to educational institutions, freedom to seek education and deliver education, academic freedom (which is closely related to freedom of expression and thought) and non-discrimination in any of the mentioned dimensions. Article 13 of the ICESCR states that higher education shall be made equally accessible to all, including that fundamental education shall be encouraged or intensified as far as possible for those persons who have not received or completed the whole period of their primary education. The CESCR has acknowledged that this provision "is the most wide-ranging and comprehensive article on the right to education in international human rights law." According to the CESCR, this right, in all its forms and levels, should be available, accessible, acceptable, and adaptable.[184] The elderly are not excluded by this provision; hence, higher education should be encouraged for the elderly.

Furthermore, the CESCR states in its General Comment 13 that the right to fundamental education is not limited by age and should be extended to older persons as stipulated in General Comment 24. It considers fundamental education an important aspect of adult education and requires states to provide all aspects of the right to education in a suitable manner for all different age groups. Additionally, in General Comment 6 the CESCR stresses the need to interpret these rights from two different perspectives, including the right of older persons to benefit from educational programs, and the right to have the knowledge and experience of older persons passed on to persons of younger generations.

[184] Right to Education (Art. 13): General Comment 13, U.N. Econ., Soc., & Cultural Rights. Comm., 21st Sess., 2, U.N. Doc. E/C.12/1999/10 (1999).

4.1.2.4 The Right to Work

States should protect workers' right (persons with impairments) to work in just and favourable working conditions through regulation of employment conditions. Access to education throughout the life course is necessary to ensure this right. Adequate work and employment are important components of the right to access to an adequate income. The right to work encompasses the right to earn a livelihood in decent working conditions and the right to individual and personal freedom and dignity.[185] Elderly persons have the right to be free from discrimination in hiring, promotion, wages, and discharge, and they have equal rights to form and to join trade unions.[186] For most of the world's older people, retirement is not an option. Those who are poor have no choice but to work, and policy makers often ignore the needs and contributions of older workers.[187] When the elderly are being productive in the society the state economy booms up. Most people will say the elderly should go on retirement and stay at home; but then if they still have the energy and can carry themselves without and support their input to the society, this should be highly appreciated else the burden of care will fall on the state or the care givers. Thus, promoting and protecting the socio-legal rights of the elderly is of the utmost importance.

The scope of the right to work for everyone according to Article 23 of UDHR includes a "free choice of employment, just and favourable conditions of work and to protection against unemployment", as well as "the right to equal pay for equal work." The provision also includes "the right to just and favourable remuneration ensuring for himself and his family an existence worthy of human dignity, and supplemented, if necessary, by other means of social protection." Elderly persons' access to these rights has not been universally defended in national laws and regulations. The elderly according to this article should have a dignified job as this will ease the burden on the care givers.

Article 6 of the ICESCR is a landmark provision establishing the scope of the right to work because it recognizes the right to work as the right of everyone to have the opportunity to gain his or her living by work that he or

185 Asbjorn, E. (1995), *The Right to Work and Rights in Work, in Economic, Social and Cultural Rights*, Dordrecht, Boston: Martinu sNijhoff Publishers, Norwell, MA, U.S.A. p.169.

186 UDHR, Article 23; CRPD, Article 27.

187 Working for Life: Making Decent Work and Pensions a Reality for Older People, Aging and Development, Help Age International, p. 2.

she freely chooses or accepts. The elderly having the free will to earn a living by working; it improves on the economy of the society which will thus have less stress in supporting the elderly financially and the state fund could then be allocated for other states projects. Further, under that same provision, states have agreed "to achieve the full realization of this right". Article 6 through 8, ICESCR follows by providing "technical and vocational guidance and training programs, policies and techniques to achieve steady economic, social and cultural development and full and productive employment under conditions safeguarding fundamental political and economic freedoms to the individual".

Also, CESCR General Comment No. 6 specifically recognizes the difficulty older persons face in finding and sustaining jobs, and advocates measures that will prevent age discrimination. In developed states, mandatory retirement at a certain age is a contentious issue. In certain circumstances it can be discriminatory, although it is often embraced by persons who would rather receive retirement benefits than continue working. In developing countries, where no such retirement benefits are generally available, conditions of work and fair income, lack of access to credit, and training are particularly salient to older workers.[188] Aware of the problems that older persons may encounter to find and keep a job, the General Comment stresses the need for measures to prevent discrimination on grounds of age in employment and occupation.

4.1.2.5 The Right to Adequate Housing

Article 11.1 of the ICESCR is delineated to the right to housing as a part of an adequate standard of living. Applying the norm requires states to respect, ensure, and fulfill this right in a manner that creates a living environment suited to the culture, skills, needs, and wishes of the people.[189] This right is complemented by the right to be protected against "arbitrary or unlawful interference" within one's home as stated in article 17.1.of ICCPR. All persons here include the elderly the socio-legal rights of the elderly are a very fundamental aspect of the society and should be treated with all consideration. The elderly deserve a living environment that is comfortable for them so as to ease their vulnerability. In most under develop countries, the elderly are often neglected by their dependence and their living condition very

188 Lindsey Judge, The Rights of Older People: International Law, Human Rights Mechanisms and the Case for New Normative Standards pg. 4 (Jan. 2009).

189 Scott Leckie, *The Right to Housing, in Economic, Social and Cultural Rights: A Textbook*113–14 (AsbjornEide et al., eds., 1995).

deplorable. States that have ratified this convention should do a follow up and monitor the elderly within the society and try to implement this article at all cost taking into consideration that the elderly are vulnerable and those they have socio-legal rights that should be protected.

According to CESCR General Comment No. 4, everyone is entitled to adequate housing, and individuals as well as families are entitled to this right "regardless of age, economic status, group or other affiliation or status and other such factors."

CESCR General Comment No. 6 affords protection to older persons with respect to housing, expanding on the need for family support; housing "must be viewed as more than mere shelter as it clearly contains a psychological and social dimension." Likewise, a report on Ageing by the Secretary General of the UN pointed out that "to the extent possible, older persons should be enabled to continue to live in their homes for as long as possible, to avoid both the physical and psychological disruptions involved in moving to an unfamiliar location," and stated that "appropriate and adequate means of transportation are also needed so that older persons can remain mobile and remain integrated into the larger community."

Furthermore, according to CESCR's General Comment No. 4, everyone is entitled to adequate housing, and individuals as well as families are entitled to this right regardless of age. The CESCR has further indicated that an initial step toward the realization of those rights is to identify the sectors of the population that should be the focus of positive state action. Throughout General Comment No. 4, the CESCR reiterated that the right to housing is an immediate right. "In essence, the obligation is to demonstrate that, in aggregate, the measures being taken are sufficient to realize the right for every individual in the shortest possible time in accordance with the maximum of available resources." The definition of available resources in relation to this right might include international assistance, such as the importance of the right to housing. Rights enforcement is a key to the immediacy of the right. According to the CESCR, "all persons should possess a degree of security of tenure which guarantees legal protection against forced eviction, harassment and other threats."[190]

190 General Comment No. 4: The Right to Adequate Housing (Art. 11 (1) of the Covenant), CESCR, E/1992/23, (Dec. 13, 1991) available at http://www.refworld.org/docid/47a7079a1. Html, accessed, 25-06-2019.

The CESCR stated that "disadvantaged groups must be accorded full and sustainable access to adequate housing resources."[191] Sustainable access for older persons is unlikely to be achieved through voucher programs alone.[192] The CESCR listed older persons as a disadvantaged group, and stated that disadvantaged persons are entitled to priority consideration in national housing schemes.

4.1.2.6 The Right to Social Protection

Social protection refers to a set of policies to help women, men and children reach or maintain an adequate standard of living and good health throughout their lives. In its most basic form it should comprise of the following: basic income security for children, providing access to nutrition, education, care and other necessary goods and services; basic income security for persons in active age who are unable to earn sufficient income, including in cases of sickness, unemployment, maternity and disability; basic income security for elderly persons; and essential health care for all, including maternity care, that meets the criteria of availability, accessibility and quality.[193]

Articles 22 of the UDHR and Article 9 ICESCR states that everyone "has the right to social security and is entitled to its realization, through national effort and international co-operation in accordance with the organization and resources of each State, of the economic, social and cultural rights indispensable for his dignity." One of the most substantial contributions to the understanding of the human rights dimension of social protection for older persons was made by the UN independent expert on the question of human rights and extreme poverty. In 2008, the independent expert indicated that extreme poverty and social exclusion constitute a violation of human dignity, and can be prevented it by adopting social security measures.[194] Typically,

[191] UN Human Rights Council, Report of the Special Rapporteur on Adequate Housing as a Component of the Right to an Adequate Standard of Living, and on the Right to Non-Discrimination in This Context, Miloon Kothari: addendum: mission to Canada A/HRC/10/7/Add.3, (9 to 22 Oct. 2007), (Feb. 17 2009) available at http://www.refworld.org/docid/49b7af2c2.htm, accessed, 01-01-2020.

[192] UN Human Rights Council, Report of the Representative of the Secretary-General on the Human Rights of Internally Displaced Persons, Walter Kälin: addendum: mission to Georgia, A/HRC/10/13/Add.2, (Feb. 13 2009).

[193] Stephen Kidd 2018; why we need social protection Copyright © United Nations, All rights reserved Printed in Thailand.

[194] Report of the independent expert on the question of human rights and extreme poverty, Arjun Sengupta , UN Human Rights Council, A/HRC/7/15, (February 28 2008).

Social Protection refers to policies and programs designed to lower poverty or some type of human misfortune while Social Security provides old- age insurance. While high-wage earners tend to pay more for benefits, they also collect higher benefit levels.

In 2010, the report of the independent expert stated that establishing or extending social security systems is more than a policy option or a means for reducing poverty; it is first-and-foremost a duty of States stemming directly from human rights norms and standards, in particular the right to social security and the right to an adequate standard of living.[195] The 2010 report also noted that when establishing or extending social pensions, the states must recognize social security as a human right and establishing appropriate legal frameworks in domestic law ensure universal access to social security, and integrate human rights principles and standards throughout the design, implementation and evaluation of social pensions.[196]

Likewise, the independent expert highlighted that as a necessary part of a rights-based approach to social pensions, the right to social security must be included in national legal frameworks. Furthermore, the social security systems should have a complaint system. According to the expert, individuals and organizations should have the right to seek, receive and impart information in a clear and transparent manner.

Through the provision of essential health care and income security along the life course, social protection plays a critical role in reducing and preventing poverty and leveling out inequalities. Countries also invest in social protection for a variety of other reasons, including supporting human development, enhancing social cohesion, strengthening their labour force and stimulating economic growth. Social protection is a human right and an integral part of the 2030 Agenda for Sustainable Development (SDG). SDG calls on all countries to provide social security to all as a means to end poverty in all its forms everywhere by 2030. Social protection is also fundamental in achieving several other SDGs. When the elderly are having social protection poverty within the society is reduced because they can be able to take care of themselves without depending on anyone.

During the second working session of the UN Open-Ended Working Group on Ageing for the purpose of strengthening the protection of the

195 Sepulveda, M. and Carlys, N. 2010 The Human Rights Approach to Social Protection Copyright by Ministry for Foreign Affairs of Finland ISBN 978-952-281-016-8.at para. 51.

196 Conclusions and Recommendations, Sepulveda Report 2010.

human rights of elderly persons, the independent expert on the question of human rights and extreme poverty sustained that "the right to social security is firmly grounded in international human rights law and that several treaties contain specific references to old age protection through social security schemes." Social protection schemes are important tools to reduce poverty and inequality. They do not only help to prevent individuals and their families from falling or remaining in poverty but also they contribute to economic growth by raising labour productivity and enhancing social stability.

Article 9 of the ICESCR describes "the right of everyone to social security, including social insurance. Regarding this, Lindsay Judged mentions that "it is clear from that Article 9 envisages non-contributory schemes for those who fall outside the ambit of contributory pensions, as well as a system of compulsory old age insurance." Article 9 outlines an entitlement and not just a benefit. Because social security payments allow older persons to procure basic needs like food and shelter, social security is an entitlement that the state must provide and protect due to its connection to the acquisition of basic needs for survival. This provision has been further elaborated in CESCR General Comment 6 and in General Comment 19 to produce a number of clearer obligations on states vis-à-vis elderly people.

As with all rights, states have a duty to uphold equality and non-discrimination, and should endeavour to eliminate sex discrimination. Elderly women already face higher risk of poverty. Elderly women may be disproportionately barred from receiving old-age contributory pensions because of years spent outside of the formal labour market, often caring for family.[197] Current standards for social security enable a decent living and are encouraged. Successful plans are currently more likely to be found in medium-income countries than low- income countries.[198]

A 2012 report of the United Nations High Commissioner for Human Rights (UNHCHR) estimated that "80% of the world's population, many of them elderly persons, lacks access to any kind of social security."[199] Also, the independent expert on human rights and poverty stated that "less than 20%

---

197 UN SG Report on Aging.

198 Report of the Special Rapporteur on Violence against Women, Its Causes and Consequences,Yakin Ertürk: addendum: mission to Tajikistan, UN Human Rights Council, A/HRC/11/6/Add.2,(Apr. 29, 2009).

199 Report to the Economic and Social Council, U.N. Econ. and Soc. Council, E/2012/5, 48, (Nov. 14 2011).

of elderly persons are covered by pensions today, and only about 25% of the labour force is currently contributing or accruing pension rights."[200]

Social protection policies play a critical role in realizing the human right to social security for all, reducing poverty and inequality, and promoting inclusive growth by boosting human capital and productivity, and by supporting domestic demand and structural transformation of national economies.

4.1.2.7 The Right to Health

Health as a human right creates a legal obligation on states to ensure access to timely, acceptable, and affordable health care of appropriate quality as well as to providing for the underlying determinants of health, such as safe and potable water, sanitation, food, housing and health-related information Everyone has the right to health. The World Health Organization defines the right to health as "a complete state of physical, mental and social well-being, and not merely the absence of disease or infirmity." States should ensure both freedoms and entitlements.

Everyone has the right to a standard of living adequate for the health and well-being of himself and of his family, including food, clothing, housing and medical care and necessary social services, and the right to security in the event of unemployment, sickness, disability, widowhood, old age or other lack of livelihood in circumstances[201] CRPD Article 25 states that States Parties recognize that persons with disabilities have the right to the enjoyment of the highest attainable standard of health without discrimination on the basis of disability. States Parties shall take all appropriate measures to ensure access for persons with disabilities to health services that are gender-sensitive, including health-related rehabilitation and The States Parties to the present Covenant recognize the right of everyone to the enjoyment of the highest attainable standard of physical and mental health[202]. According to HelpAge International, the area of health care is a domain in which elderly persons are frequently subject to discrimination, either by being denied access to services, or receiving substandard or insufficient care on account

---

200 Sepulveda, 2010 The Human Rights Approach to Social Protection Copyright by Ministry for Foreign Affairs of Finland ISBN 978-952-281-016-8.

201 The Universal Declaration of Human Right (UDHR) Article 25.

202 ICESCR Article 12.

of their age.[203] States are required to give particular attention to securing the right to health, ensuring equality and non-discrimination.[204] A right to basic health care means that the government is morally obligated to do all within its means to ensure that medically necessary care is accessible and affordable to all and to enact a health care policy worthy of the country's highest moral principles.

Aging can present a significant challenge to achieving effective health care.[205] Health systems should be responsive to the particular needs of elderly persons.[206] As stated by the United Nations High Commissioner for Human Rights in the context of health and end-of-life care, dignity and respect for all human rights is the key for the well-being of older persons.[207]

The right to health for all people means that everyone should have access to the health services they need, when and where they need them, without suffering financial hardship. No one should get sick and die just because they are poor, or because they cannot access the health services they need.

The General Assembly on the follow-up to the Second World Assembly on Ageing, pointed out that elderly persons are entitled to the enjoyment of a satisfactory standard of physical and mental health, with due attention to preventive, curative, rehabilitative and long- term care. Likewise, the independent expert on human rights and extreme poverty ascertained that without this, many may fall into a vicious cycle where poor health engenders poverty and poverty engenders poor health. The independent expert Sepulveda also underlined that social pensions should be planned and implemented in close coordination with other initiatives aimed at ensuring the enjoyment of the right the highest attainable standard of health by elderly persons, and in

203 Help Age Position Paper (Convention), 2009.

204 UN Human Rights Council, Report of the Special Rapporteur on the Right of Everyone to the Enjoyment of the Highest Attainable Standard of Physical and Mental Health, Anand Grover, A/HRC/11/12, (Mar. 31 2009) available at http://www.refworld.org/docid/49faf7652.html, accessed, 20-02-2020. see also UN Human Rights Council, Report of the Special Rapporteur on the Right of Everyone to the Enjoyment of the Highest Attainable Standard of Physical and Mental Health, Paul Hunt: addendum: Missions to the World Bank and the International Monetary Fund in Washington, D.C. (20 October 2006) and Uganda (4–7 February 2007), A/HRC/7/11/Add.2, (Mar. 5 2008) available at http://www.refworld.org/docid/47da904c2.html accessed on 12 November 2019.

205 U.N. General Assembly, Implementation of General Assembly Resolution 60/251 (May 31 2007).

206 Report of the Special Rapporteur on the Right of Everyone to the Enjoyment of the Highest Attainable Standard of Physical and Mental Health: A/HRC/7/11, 31 at 42 (Jan. 2008) http://www.who.int/medicines/areas/human_rights/A_HRC_7_11.pdf, accessed 12-11-2019.

207 Report of the United Nations High Commissioner for Human Rights, U.N. Econ. and Soc. Council, E/2012/51 53 (Apr. 20 2012).

fact, providing pensions grants an opportunity for better articulation of health services to other government program.

According to the Report of the United Nations High Commissioner for Human Rights of April 2012, elderly persons may face severe health conditions, often overextended periods of time, and are confronted with profound psychosocial and spiritual questions as they face illness or death and physical pain. Persons who live with chronic pain are more likely to suffer from depression or anxiety, according to certain studies.[208] Similarly, the General Assembly has also indicated that depression is known to be common among elderly persons, although in developing countries, precise data are scarce and depression, loneliness and anxiety may arise as a result of major life changes such as the death of a spouse or a sudden decline in health and it "is also considered to be a main factor in explaining the surge in suicide rates among persons aged 75 and over."[209] As the body ages, it becomes prone to medical conditions. Ageing cannot be prevented, but we can learn how to deal with arising conditions for great health of our loved ones. Most health concerns for the elderly are memory loss, dementia and Alzheimer's disease, among others. When the elderly right to health is protected they are more productive to the society.

Article 12 of the ICESCR recognizes "the right of everyone to the highest attainable standard of physical and mental health." It goes on to highlight particular priorities states should consider, including "the prevention, treatment and control of epidemic, endemic, occupational and other diseases" and "the creation of conditions which would assure to all medical service and medical attention in the event of sickness."[210] States should have reviewed mechanisms in place to address violations of the right to health. In addition, states should maintain adequate training standards for health care professionals. For elderly persons, this might encourage the mainstreaming of geriatric medicine in medical training and professional programs.

In CESCR General Comment No. 14, which addresses health, there are four core aspects to the right to health. Availability refers to the sufficient quantity and sustainable quality of health care facilities, goods, services

208 Report of the United Nations High Commissioner for Human Rights, U.N. Econ. and Soc. Council, E/2012/51 54 (Apr. 20 2012).

209 U.N. General Assembly, Follow-up to the Second World Assembly on Ageing A/67/188, (July 26 2012) 33.

210 Lindsey Judge, The Rights of Older People: International Law, Human Rights Mechanisms and the Case for New Normative Standards, pg. 6 (Jan. 2009).

and programs. Accessibility includes the notions of non-discrimination, and physical, economical, and informational accessibility. Acceptability refers to cultural appropriateness, including gender sensitivities and data confidentiality. Finally, quality refers to the scientifically and medically appropriate production of medical goods, services, facilities, and drugs. The CESCR reaffirms paragraphs 34 and 35 of General Comment No. 6, which reiterates the need for preventative, curative and rehabilitative health treatment for elderly persons, including rehabilitative measures. Likewise, the CESCR reiterates the recommendations of the Vienna International Plan of Action on Ageing, which took a similar comprehensive view of all stages of health. Like any younger person, the elderly shop, they use services (which employ people), and they pay taxes. They also volunteer; in fact, many organizations would be hard pressed to function without their older volunteers. Like any other group of vulnerable, the elderly do have socio- legal rights that have to be protected through international law and implemented at the national level. Though there is no specific convention that fully covers the socio-legal rights of the elderly, these rights have been spread throughout various international conventions, treaties and recommendation. This has caused the implementation at the national level difficult; thus there is a continuous violation of their rights within the society. It will be of relevance to this work for us to look at the rights of the elderly as members of other vulnerable groups.

4.2 Right of Elderly Persons as Members of other Vulnerable Groups

Vulnerability is the degree to which a population, individual or organization is unable to anticipate, cope with, resist and recover from the impacts of disasters, environmental health in emergencies and disasters.[211] We cannot accurately predict which groups of people will be most affected by future emergencies. However, recent events have shown that some characteristics of older adults put them at greater risk of illness and death during many types of emergencies.[212] For example, older adults may have impaired mobility, diminished sensory awareness, multiple chronic health conditions, and social and economic limitations all of which can impair their ability to prepare for,

211 World Health Organization Report of 2002.

212 Centers for Disease Control and Prevention. Identifying Vulnerable Older Adults and Legal Options for Increasing Their Protection During All-Hazards Emergencies: A Cross-Sector Guide for States and Communities. Atlanta: U.S. Department of Health and Human Services; 2012.

respond to, and adapt during emergencies. An emergency or disaster also can disrupt vital support systems that older adults rely on. For many older adults, independent living is made possible only with help from friends, family, and in-home services that provide meals, home-based health care, and help with the activities of daily living.

As mentioned by the General Assembly regarding the realization of the right to health, General Comment No. 14 considers older persons to be a group especially vulnerable to human rights violations. The condition of vulnerability requires special attention to ensure the necessary autonomy to guarantee individual choice of models of care, to the extent possible.[213]

Equality and non-discrimination are at the core of the recognition of the heightened need for state protection of vulnerable groups" rights. Historical discrimination, diminished representation in decision-making and barriers to political participation are all factors for singling out a group as vulnerable. The language of vulnerability is a common thread in human rights discourse.[214] The argument that elderly persons should be recognized as a distinct group requiring special attention and care is not a new one by any means. However, the recognition has gained increasing attention in the past few years. According to the General Assembly a study undertaken by HelpAge International in 2010 found that only 93 out of 1,912 humanitarian assistance projects surveyed explicitly addressed elderly persons as a vulnerable group.[215]

It is worth noting that not all elderly persons are vulnerable in the same way, for example, not all children or persons with disabilities are considered to be in a situation of exclusion or marginalization by merely belonging to a "vulnerable group". But, in general, it is recognized that they may need special protection in many challenging circumstances in which their inherent vulnerability exposes them to more hardship than other groups. It is also important that the classification of vulnerability is identified, in a specific context, as an important if sometimes socially constructed source of discrimination, isolation, poverty, and disempowerment. The conventions on the rights of women, children, and

213 U.N. General Assembly, Thematic Study on the Realization of the Right to Health of Older Persons by Special Rapporteur on the Right of Everyone to the Enjoyment of the Highest Attainable Standard of Physical and Mental Health, Anand Grover, A/HRC/18/37 28 (July 4 2011).

214 UN Human Rights Council, Compilation Prepared by the Office of the High Commissioner for Human Rights, in accordance with paragraph 15(b) of the Annex to Human Rights Council Resolution 5/1 - Bahrain, A/HRC/WG.6/1/BHR/2, (Mar. 14 2008).

215 U.N. Secretary General, Second Review and Appraisal of the Madrid International Plan of Action on Ageing 2002, E/CN.5/2012/5 63, (Nov. 3 2011).

persons with disabilities, among others, were established on the recognition that these groups needed special assistance to ensure the protection and fulfillment of the rights enshrined in existing conventions for these persons. The United Nations General Assembly emphasizes non- discrimination as a part of the UDHR, and the legal frameworks for the protection of vulnerable groups' rights to employment, food, social development, social integration, cultural participation and accessibility.

Multiple discriminations can be the source of compounded violations of elderly persons" rights, if we consider that older persons also make up a large portion of all vulnerable groups.[216] For example, the Special Rapporteur on the situation of human rights and fundamental freedoms of indigenous persons has noted that government reparations for wrongful actions against indigenous populations can and should be expedited for elderly persons, who are more likely to face circumstances of extreme need.[217] The HR Council in this guise recommends the continued raising of awareness among traditional communities about the protection and promotion of the rights of elderly people, particularly the multiple discriminations faced by elderly women[218] and other vulnerable group. The Human Rights Committee has recommended human rights education in accordance with Articles 2(1) and 26 of the ICCPR where vulnerable groups' rights are being exploited.

The CESCR notes that economic and social disparities have particular effect on vulnerable groups, including, expressly, elderly persons,[219] who are particularly prone to unequal distribution of poverty in the first place.[220] It further urges efforts for greater economic, social and cultural rights for all vulnerable groups including, expressly, older persons.[221] The CESCR

216 General Comment 15 (Twenty-ninth session, 2002): The Right to Water (arts. 11 and 12 of the Covenant), ICESCR E/2003/22 (2002) 120 at 16(h), General Comment 5, and General Comment 6.

217 UN Human Rights Council, UN Human Rights Council: Addendum to the Report of the Special Rapporteur on the Situation of Human Rights and Fundamental Freedoms of Indigenous People, Study Regarding Best Practices Carried out to Implement the Recommendations Contained in the Annual Reports of the Special Rapporteur, A/HRC/4/32/Add.4, (Feb. 26, 2007), available at http://www.refworld.org/docid/4623896f2.html accessed on the 27 November 2019 access on the 15 December 2019.

218 UN Human Rights Council, Report of the Working Group on the Universal Periodic Review - Burkina Faso, A/HRC/10/80; A/HRC/WG.6/3/L.12, (Jan. 7 2009).

219 Guatemala, ICESCR, E/1997/22 29 at 127 (1996).

220 Report of the UN Committee on Economic, Social and Cultural Rights, Twenty-eighth and Twenty-ninth Sessions (29 April - 17 May 2002, 11–29 November 2002) CESCR, E/2003/22;E/C.12/2002/13, 39 at 221 (June 23 2003).

221 Australia, ICESCR, E/1994/23 36 at 159 (1993) http://www.bayefsky.com/general/e_1994_23.pdf.

encourages participation, and condemns legislation restricting the rights of vulnerable groups based on public opinion trends.

A lack of state action to combat discrimination threatens vulnerable groups.[222] The HR Council emphasizes state facilitation of a policy of participation as a remedy for curtailed civil, cultural, economic, political, and social rights, and poverty in its Forum on Minority Issues.[223] The Convention Against Torture (CAT) emphasizes the elimination of police discrimination against all vulnerable groups, as well as their torture and ill treatment, and recommends steps to ensure the physical integrity of vulnerable groups.[224] The United Nations Department of Economic and Social Affairs notes the need for equality and non-discrimination for vulnerable groups in its 2005 Report on the World Social Situation. In Croatia's Working Group Report, the Committee on the Elimination of Racial Discrimination (CERD) emphasized the need for continuous monitoring of vulnerable or disadvantaged groups within minority communities to identify areas for improvement, and efforts targeted for the most vulnerable groups so that the government can measure and act accordingly.[225]

The Third Committee of the GA also asserted in the 2009 Final Report its ongoing commitment to vulnerable groups, reducing vulnerability of older persons, and developing cooperatives to enable the meeting of social service needs for vulnerable groups and, expressly, older persons. Similarly, the UN Secretary General observed a number of actions pertinent to vulnerable groups. This included the need for targeted assistance, the need for improved law and social development programs that work toward social integration,[226] and they encouraged UN bodies to monitor the situations of vulnerable groups.[227] Individual state comments during the Upper Periodical Report UPRs (Popular

222 Human Rights Committee Annual Report to the U.N. General Assembly, Romania, ICCPR, A/49/40 vol. I1742U.N. General Assembly, Human Rights Council Forum on Minority Issues Second session Geneva, 12–13 November 2009 Note by the Independent Expert on Minority Issues, Gay McDougall, on Minorities and Effective Political Participation.

223 U.N. General Assembly, Human Rights Council Forum on Minority Issues Second session Geneva, 12–13 November 2009 Note by the Independent Expert on Minority Issues, Gay McDougall, on Minorities and Effective Political Participation.

224 Greece, CAT, A/56/44 (2001) 38 at 88.

225 Final Report of the Third Committee A/64/432 (2009) *available at* http://daccess-dds-ny.un.org/doc/UNDOC/GEN/N09/627/09/PDF/N0962709.pdf?OpenElement accessed 2-03-2019.

226 Report of the Secretary-General on the implementation of the outcome of the World Summit for Social Development and of the twenty-fourth special session of the General Assembly A/60/117 (July 13 2005).

227 U.N. Secretary General, Effective Promotion of the Declaration on the Rights of Persons Belonging to National or Ethnic, Religious, and Linguistic Minorities A/60/333 (Sep. 6, 2005).

Republican Union) often include praise for or recognition of shortcomings in connection with being a party to individual human rights treaties, individual states' domestic legal standards, mechanisms and institutions to monitor implementation and efforts to protect vulnerable groups. These state comments have included praise for preventing discrimination against vulnerable groups, and note the need of state action to protect human rights of vulnerable groups, including, expressly, elderly persons.[228]

4.2.1 The Rights of Elderly Refugees and other Persons in Emergencies

Older refugee women and men face particular challenges during the different phases of displacement (flight, displacement, resettlement, and reintegration). UNHCR staff and partners need to ensure that the rights of elderly persons concerned are met without discrimination. To do this, teams should develop a thorough understanding of both the needs and capacities of elderly persons in displaced populations. Systematic application of the Age, Gender and Diversity (AGD) approach is central to achieving UNHCR"s commitment to make sure that older persons have access to, and are included in, all protection activities and durable solutions.

United Nations Convention on the Rights of Persons with Disabilities (CRPD) in Article 11 provides that persons with disabilities, as all people, have equal rights to humanitarian relief following a natural disaster or conflicts. Elderly persons are also entitled to that right, on equal footing with others. Old age can result in decreased mobility, sight, hearing, and muscle strength, as well as in greater vulnerability to heat and cold.[229]

Humanitarian actors have a duty to recognize the limited mobility of many groups. As the UNHCR guidelines for best practices regarding elderly persons in disaster and humanitarian crisis state, "The first key principle of good practice is to be aware of the presence of older persons in an emergency

---

228 UN Human Rights Council, Report of the Working Group on the Universal Periodic Review - Bangladesh, A/HRC/WG.6/4/L.4, A/HRC/11/18, (Mar. 3 2009), available at http://www.refworld.org/docid/49f964eb0.html; UN Human Rights Council, Report of the Working Group on the Universal Periodic Review - Chile, A/HRC/12/10; A/HRC/WG.6/5/L.9, (June 4,2009) available at http://www.refworld.org/docid/4a9cdb920.html. (Czech Republic urging the approval of a draft refugee law according special attention to vulnerable groups to prevent discrimination).

229 Humanitarian Action and Older Persons - An essential brief for humanitarian actors, Initiated by WHO and HelpAge International at the request of the Inter-Agency Standing Committee (IASC) Working Group, Inter Agency Standing Comm., 3 (2008).

and take active steps to locate and identify them."[230] The guidelines also point out that limited mobility can create severe problems for older persons in crises.[231] Elderly persons are at risk of exclusion from protection and assistance programmes if humanitarian actors do not fully understand their needs, and do not involve them actively in decisions that concern their wellbeing. It cannot be presumed that they will always benefit from family assistance programmes, or from family or community support networks. Staff and partners need to deliberately adopt an inclusive and participatory approach. Through consultation processes (such as Participatory Assessments), elderly women and men can help to design and implement programmes that really meet their needs, and can be supported to do what they can to improve their own situation. Consultation and participation through all phases, in crises and protracted situations, are essential.[232] Older women and men will experience displacement differently, based on their cultural and socio-economic status. Offices must invest the time and effort to fully understand these gender differences so they can be taken into consideration when designing protection responses. According to research done by HelpAge International, four main problems were identified: incapacity to gain access to essential services; physical limitations; lack of transportation; and the loss of mobility aids, prostheses and glasses in the emergency.[233]

Article 4 of the ICCPR provides for the possibility of derogating from certain Covenant obligations in time of public emergency which threatens the life of the nation and the existence of which is officially proclaimed. Article 4 of the ICCPR stipulates that in time of public emergency state parties may take measures derogating from certain of their obligations under the ICCPR. According to that provision, however, certain rights are non- derogable. Article 4 of the ICCPR provides for the possibility of derogating from certain Covenant obligations "in time of public emergency which threatens the life of the nation and the existence of which is officially proclaimed." When faced with situations of armed conflict, the HRC will necessarily examine whether these state parties complied with all of their ICCPR obligations and whether they have satisfied the conditions of Article 4 of the ICCPR. Any derogation

230 HelpAge International, Older People In Disasters and Humanitarian Crises, UNHCR, 3available at http://www.refworld.org/pdfd/4124b9f44.pdf. Accessed 20-6-2019.

231 Ibid. at p. 5.

232 United Nations High Commissioner for Refugees 2013 Working With older Persons in Forced displacement 1202 Geneva, Switzerland.

233 HelpAge International, Older People In Disasters and Humanitarian Crises.

must be immediately brought to the attention of State parties through the intermediary of the Secretary-General and further notification is required upon the termination of the derogation.

The Fourth Geneva Convention Relative to the Protection of Civilian Persons in Time of War defines humanitarian protections for civilians in a war zone, and prohibits the practice of total war.[234] Article 14 further states that in time of peace, and after the outbreak of hostilities, states may establish in their own territory and, if the need arises in occupied areas, hospitals, and safety zones the means to protect from the effects of war, wounded, sick and as well as, *inter alia*, aged persons. Additionally, in accordance to Article 17, the parties to the conflict shall endeavour to conclude local agreements for the removal from besieged or encircled areas, of, *inter alia*, aged persons, and for the passage of ministers of all religions, medical personnel, and medical equipment on their way to such areas. A Report of the UNHCR emphasizes the obligation of all states and parties to armed conflicts to protect civilians in accordance with international humanitarian law, and invites states to promote a culture of protection, taking into account the particular needs of, among others, elderly persons.[235]

Grounded in Article 14 of the Universal Declaration of human rights 1948, which recognizes the right of persons to seek asylum from persecution in other countries, the United Nations Convention relating to the Status of Refugees, adopted in 1951, is the centerpiece of international refugee protection today.[236] The 1951 Convention endorses a single definition of the term "refugee" in Article1. A refugee, according to the Convention, is someone who is unable or unwilling to return to their country of origin owing to a well-founded fear of being persecuted for reasons of race, religion, nationality, membership of a particular social group, or political opinion. The rights of elderly refugees are specifically recognized in the Convention relating to the Status of Refugees, in particular the provisions related to the labour legislation and social security.[237] According to Article 24, the state parties shall guarantee to refugees lawfully staying in their territory the same treatment as is accorded

234 Geneva Convention relative to the Protection of Civilian Persons in Time of War, Int"l Comm. Of the Red Cross (ICRC) 75 UNTS 287 (Aug. 12, 1949).

235 U.N. General Assembly, Report of the United Nations High Commissioner for Refugees, Questions Relating to Refugees, Returnees and Displaced Persons and Humanitarian Questions, A/59/498 (Dec. 2 2004).

236 United Nations General Assembly resolution 429(V)of 14 December 1950.

237 U.N. High Commissioner for Refugees, Convention and Protocol Relating to the Status of Refugees 1951.

to nationals in respect of, among others, social security including legal provisions in respect of old age, death, unemployment, family responsibilities and any other contingency, which, according to national laws or regulations, is covered by a social security.

UNHCR notes the particular need for ongoing protection of vulnerable groups within refugee groups.[238] Elderly internally displaced persons (IDP"s) in West Africa have been identified as requiring special attention.[239] The deprivation of elderly persons is one clear negative impact of food crises. There, immediate food needs are closely related to the shortage of fertilizers and fuel.[240] Furthermore, the United Nations Office for the Coordination of Humanitarian Affairs (UNOCHA) Guiding Principles on Internal Displacement, in Principle 4, indicates that:

> *Certain internally displaced persons, such as children, especially unaccompanied minors, expectant mothers, mothers with young children, female heads of household, persons with disabilities and elderly persons, shall be entitled to protection and assistance required by their condition and to treatment which takes into account their special needs.*[241]

The humanitarian community is increasingly aware of the crisis of internal displacement which affects over 20 million people worldwide. While responsibility for the protection of IDPs rests first and foremost with national governments and local authorities, it is important for the international community to see how best it can contribute to enhancing the protection of IDPs in conflict and crisis situations. We must also design humanitarian assistance in such a way that it will promote the protection of IDPs[242].

---

238 U.N. General Assembly, Report of the United Nations High Commissioner for Refugees, Questions Relating to Refugees, Returnees and Displaced Persons and Humanitarian Questions, A/59/498 (Dec. 2 2004).

239 UN Human Rights Council, UN Human Rights Council: Addendum to the Report of the Representative of the Secretary-General on the Human Rights of Internally Displaced Persons, First Regional Conference on Internal Displacement in West Africa (Abuja - 26–28 April 2006), A/HRC/4/38/Add.4, (Feb. 20 2007).

240 UN Human Rights Council, Report of the Special Rapporteur on the Situation of Human Rights in the Democratic People"s Republic of Korea, VititMuntarbhorn, A/HRC/10/18, at no. 49 (Feb. 24 2009).

241 UNOCHA, Guiding Principles on Internal Displacement (2004).

242 Ibid. Pg 4.

Priority should be given to elderly persons in emergencies for food relief.[243] The right of elderly persons to have their basic needs addressed in disasters must be secured by the state concerned, with its ultimate responsibility to protect the rights of its people.[244]

The particular vulnerability of women and children, as well as elderly persons and persons with disabilities, among refugees and displaced persons, including exposure to discrimination, sexual exploitation and abuse, physical abuse, violence and exploitation and the recruitment and use of children by parties to armed conflict in violation of applicable international law, and in this regard acknowledging the importance of preventing, responding to and addressing sexual and gender-based violence as well as violations and abuses committed against refugee, returnee and displaced children[245] is something states should take seriously and ensure protection to these group of persons especially the elderly.

The special needs of older IDPs should be identified and addressed in all phases of displacement.[246] Among the internally displaced, especially during winter time in Europe and America access to adequate housing is extremely important for elderly persons. It is recommended that states should relax naturalization requirements, in particular language proficiency exams, for older persons.[247]

Elderly displaced persons have more serious health problems than the non-displaced due to problems of adaptation, poverty, and changing family care dynamics, limiting intergenerational support, among others. UNHCR has called for a review of health services for elderly populations with non-

---

243 UN Human Rights Council, Report of the Special Rapporteur on the Situation of Human Rights in the Democratic People's Republic of Korea, VititMuntarbhorn, A/HRC/10/18, at no. 11 (Feb. 24 2009).

244 UN Human Rights Council, Report of the Special Rapporteur on the Situation of Human Rights in Myanmar, TomásOjea Quintana, on the implementation of Council resolutions S-5/1 and 6/33,A/HRC/8/12, (Jun. 3 2008).

245 Report of the United Nations High Commissioner for Refugees, questions relating to refugees, returnees and displaced persons and humanitarian questions 21 September 2018, Draft resolution I paragraph 5.

246 UN Human Rights Council, UN Human Rights Council: Addendum to the Report of the Representative of the Secretary-General on the Human Rights of Internally Displaced Persons, First Regional Conference on Internal Displacement in West Africa (Abuja - 26–28 April 2006),A/HRC/4/38/Add.4, (Feb. 20 2007).

247 UN Human Rights Council, Report of the Special Rapporteur on Contemporary Forms of Racism, Racial Discrimination, Xenophobia and Related Intolerance, DoudouDiène: addendum: mission to Latvia, A/HRC/7/19/Add.3, no. 88 (Mar. 5 2008).

communicable diseases in current UNHCR health policy.[248] In addition, UNHCR has sought to highlight issues of age-based violence, which are both a criminal and a health issue.[249] It has created self-reliance and income generation projects for West African refugees considering age,[250] and has created age-sensitive support for local integration. It reported in 2006 that it was monitoring new refugee laws to see that they are in line with international protection standards and take into account gender and age specific needs.[251] UNHCR also requires consideration for the needs of elderly persons who are returning refugees in order to ensure that they receive adequate protection, assistance and care throughout the repatriation and initial reintegration process.[252]

In its Policy on Older Refugees, 2000, UNHCR states that elderly refugees will always have special needs,[253] and affirmed that the policy on elderly refugees has been formulated with the hope that future efforts on behalf of older persons will have become so well integrated into all aspects of protection and program planning and implementation.[254] The Policy also indicates that the components of a policy aimed at elderly refugees shall be pre- requisites for ensuring their participation and well-being.[255] The Report further affirms the importance of age in ensuring the participation of refugees and other persons in the planning and implementation of programs and affirms the importance of giving a priority to addressing discrimination.[256]

The Report also called upon the governments concerned to focus attention and efforts on upholding protection to ensure proper consideration of the specific needs of elderly persons. Additionally, the Report called for emphasis on the age and gender sensitive approaches and "support to boost the integration capacity of various groups with special needs", including elderly refugees, and it also encouraged UNHCR "to develop and apply appropriate

248 Public Health Equity in Refugee and Other Displaced Persons Settings, Evaluation Report, 14 (Apr. 2010).
249 UNHCR Global Report 2008, Liberia 2, UN High Commissioner for Refugees (UNHCR), UNHCR Global Report 2008, Liberia, (June 2009).
250 UNHCR Global Report 2007, West Africa.
251 UNHCR Global Report 2006 Sub-regional Report for Southern South America.
252 Ibid.
253 UN High Commissioner for Refugees (UNHCR), UNHCR""s Policy on Older Refugees, EC/50/ SC/CRP.13, Annex II, (April 19 2000).
254 Ibid.pg 4.
255 Ibid.pg 5.
256 Ibid.pg 4.

standards and indicators that account for age and gender considerations in local integration and self-reliance programs."[257]

4.2.2 The Rights of Older Women

Elderly women are often stigmatized because of their gender and age. The majority of elderly persons are women because of their longer life expectancy. Elderly women face abuse and mistreatment, age-related discrimination, do not access inheritance and suffer economic exploitation.[258] Elderly women are disproportionately disadvantaged: despite making up an ever-greater proportion of the population, they are often poorer than elderly men. This is a result of gendered discrimination patterns throughout their lives.[259] This has led to social imbalanced and if care is not taken to close up the gaps elderly women will still be violated on a daily bases. On average, elderly women accumulate less wealth than men. It is more difficult for them to find work and they are paid less than elderly men. By the time women have reached old age, many have experienced multiple disadvantages resulting from biases to gender, widowhood, and old age, among others. Such situations lead many older women into poverty.[260] Further examination of multiple discriminations across the life course has been encouraged by the Report of the independent expert on the question of human rights and extreme poverty, in her March 2010 report on social security.[261] This Report highlights that:

> *The majority of older women are excluded from formal social security and health insurance schemes as these are linked to paid, formal-sector employment. In developing countries, the great majority of women work all their lives in the informal sector or unpaid activities. In developed countries too, older women are more likely than men to be poor at old age.*[262]

---

257 Ibid.pg 5.

258 G.A. Res. 65/182, (Aug. 1–4 2011).

259 Follow-Up to the Second World Assembly on Ageing: Report of the Secretary-General, Submitted to the United Nations General Assembly, A/64/127, 49 (July 2009).

260 Chung Working Paper 2010 para. 16.

261 UN Human Rights Council, Report of the Independent Expert on the Question of Human Rights and Extreme Poverty, A/HRC/14/31, (Mar. 31 2010).

262 Magdalena Sepúlveda Carmona Report of the Special Rapporteur on extreme poverty and human rights, 11 March 2013.

The exclusion schemes of the elderly women are a gross violation of their socio-legal rights which need to be protected by the state at all possible cost. The ICCPR recognizes in its Article 3 that all civil and political rights set forth in the covenant are to be enjoyed equally by men and women. Also, United Nations Convention on the Rights of Persons with Disabilities CRPD contains special provisions for women, in particular Article 6 which provides that "state parties recognize that women and girls with disabilities are subject to multiple discriminations, and in this regard shall take measures to ensure the full and equal enjoyment by them of all human rights and fundamental freedoms." Nearly one in five women lives with disabilities[263]. However, disabled women and girls remain at the margins of decision-making and their specific needs were largely invisible until recently, both to advocates of women's rights and disability rights. In humanitarian contexts, women and girls with disabilities face even more discrimination, adding to an already heightened risk of violence and exploitation

To ensure respect for elderly women's right to social security, the CESCR suggests that states should refrain from discriminating against women who choose to stay at home to raise a family. This require states to acknowledge time spent at home as a homemaker as work experience when evaluating women for employment opportunities. Such decisions will assist in the amelioration of poverty among elderly women. To ensure this right, particularly in connection with Article 9 of the ICESCR, the CESCR provides that states should provide non-contributory old-age benefits or other assistance for all persons.[264] This benefit would be given, regardless of sex, to those without adequate resources upon reaching a prescribed age specified in national legislation.[265] To fulfill this right, the CESCR stipulates that states should promote the need for more men to stay at home to raise families.

The Convention on the Elimination of All Forms of Discrimination against Women CEDAW in Article 1 elaborates on the term "discrimination against women" as any exclusion or restriction made on the basis of sex which has the effect or purpose of impairing or nullifying the recognition, enjoyment or exercise by women irrespective of their marital status, on a basis of equality of men and women, of human rights and fundamental freedoms in the political, economic, social, cultural, civil or any other field. It is clear that the

---

263 World Health Organization (WHO) and the World Bank (2011). World Report on Disability.

264 The Economic, Social, and Cultural Rights of Older Persons (Thirteenth Session, 1995) Comm. on Econ. Soc. and Cultural Rights, U.N. Doc. E/1996/22, 21. (1996).

265 Ibid.Pg 2.

CEDAW Convention does not only require the absence of a discriminatory legal framework, but also laws and policies must not be discriminatory in effect. In other words, the CEDAW Convention requires both substantive and formal equality, non-discrimination and empowerment of women, and therefore recognizes that formal equality alone is insufficient for a state to meet its obligation and requires measures to address both direct and indirect discrimination to achieve substantive equality between men and women[266]. The CEDAW Convention provides strong standards on equality and non-discrimination for all women. It also provides critical normative standards that are intrinsically linked to the Agenda 2030 for sustainable development such as those related to food, education health, housing, non- discrimination, legal capacity, political participation and equal family relations. The adoption of a development framework based on these standards for the full enjoyment of human rights of women enshrined in the CEDAW Convention must underpin the principle of "ensuring that no one it is left behind".

With regard to older women, Article 11 of the CEDAW guarantees "the right to social security, particularly in cases of retirement, unemployment, sickness, invalidity and old age and other incapacity to work, as well as the right to paid leave." As for other financial assistance, Article 13 of the CEDAW covers economic and social benefits, including the right to family benefits, bank loans, mortgages, and other forms of financial credit. Social security for every elderly person is a fundamental right that states should promote and protect. And elderly without any form of social security especially the rural woman is a disheartening situation. The CEDAW also acknowledges an especially vulnerable position of rural women requiring state parties to take particular measures to ensure the application of these provisions. This include their participation in the development planning, access to adequate health care facilities and equal access to economic opportunities through employment and enjoy adequate living conditions. All these have gone a long to pave the way for the socio-legal recognition of the rights of elderly people particularly the elderly women. As for marriage and family life, the CEDAW in Article 16 also emphasizes the obligation of the state parties to "eliminate discrimination against women in all matters relating to marriage and family relations." The fundamental equality of the sexes comes in the form of marriage and family relations as well. Women for almost all of recorded history in most societies

266 United Nations Sustainable Development Goal Committee on the Elimination of Discrimination against Women (CEDAW) 2016.

have been considered the property of the family, the community, the society, and, in fact, the religion. Due to the fact most of these rights are spread across different conventions. Protection and implementation is a cause for concern in the protection of the socio-legal rights of the elderly.

In CEDAW General Recommendation No 24 on health, the CEDAW Committee stated that "there are societal factors, which are determinative of the health status of women and men, and for that reason, special attention should be given to the health needs and rights of women belonging to vulnerable and disadvantaged groups," such as, *inter alia*, "older women."[267] Elderly women occupy a majority of elderly people and to an extent when their socio-legal rights are protected, the society to them turns to be a happy place for healthy aging.

Human rights experts addressing the CEDAW Committee regarding its General Recommendation No. 25, have indicated that, it recognizes that discrimination against women can be compounded by other types of exclusion including age, and allows states to take temporary special measures to overcome the entrenched nature of discrimination such women face.[268] It noted that certain groups of women might also suffer from multiple forms of discrimination based on additional grounds such as, *inter alia*, age. The recommendation stated that "such discrimination may affect these groups of women primarily, or to a different degree or in different ways than men. State parties may need to take specific temporary special measures to eliminate such multiple forms of discrimination against women and its compounded negative impact on them."[269]

In recent years, there has been growing pressure on the CEDAW Committee to pay closer attention to the rights of elderly women. Consequently, in 2010, the CEDAW Committee adopted the landmark General Recommendation No. 27 on the rights of elderly women and protection of their human rights. The General Recommendation explores the relationship between the rights protected by CEDAW and aging. It also acknowledges the multiple forms

267 ICESCR (Twentieth session, 1999): Article 2: Women and Health, A/54/38/Rev.1 part I 3 at 6 (1999) also, UN Committee on the Elimination of Discrimination Against Women (CEDAW), CEDAW General Recommendation No. 24: Article 12 of the Convention (Women and Health), A/54/38/Rev.1, chap. I, (1999).

268 Lindsey Judge, Jan. 2009 The Rights of Older People: International Law, Human Rights Mechanisms and the Case for New Normative Standards pg. 9.

269 Report of the Committee on the Elimination of Discrimination against Women: Thirtieth session, UN Comm. on the Elimination of Discrimination Against Women (CEDAW), (12–30 January 2004), Thirty-first session (6–23 July 2004), Thirtieth session, (2004): Article 4, Paragraph 1: Temporary Special Measures, A/59/38 part I 78 at 12. (2004).

of discrimination that women face across their lives, outlines the scope of the state obligations under CEDAW with respect to the protection of elderly women and includes policy recommendations. Ultimately, the General Recommendation provides guidance to states by including the situation of elderly women in their periodic reports to the Committee. However, this guidance has not yet resulted in the routine inclusion of the situation of elderly women in reports.

Cultural practices of early marriage for women, in addition to their longer life expectancy, creates a situation in which women are more likely to be widowed than men, which in turn puts elderly women at higher risk of poverty. The CESCR expressed concern about the problem of the abandonment of elderly women and strongly recommended that the state party "undertake effective public education measures, including awareness-raising programs designed to eliminate gender based prejudices and traditional practices that are harmful to women."[270] Land and inheritance rights in many countries deny women their right to own and keep property.[271] The CEDAW Committee has also denounced this problem and documented that widows in some countries are victims of "property grabbing," as a result of the application of domestic statutory or customary laws.[272] Witchcraft allegations and violence against elderly women are usually linked to disputes over property ownership and inheritance. This can lead to impoverishment, abuse, violence and even murder. At the international level, a lot of attention has been given to the protection of their socio-legal rights of elderly women. Though these rights are well articulated in the CEDAW, there is still a greater problem with the implementation due to the fact that there are no appropriate monitoring bodies that submit report on cases of violation. These still leave the socio-legal rights of the elderly heavily unprotected. We have been studying the rights of elderly persons as members of other vulnerable group; it will be important for us now to examine the rights of elderly persons with disabilities.

---

270 China, ICESCR, E/2006/22 25 at 148 and 178 (2005).

271 HelpAge International, Ageing and Development, Issue 26, (Sep. 2009) HelpAge International, Final Evaluation Report of the Older Women Inheritance Rights Project, (May 2008) (In T anzania, for example, 77% of the cases on disputes over inheritance and land rights were brought by older women).

272 Committee, General Recommendation No. 27 on older women and protection of their human rights, note 558, para. 26.

4.3 Conclusion

Cameroon has made progress in recognizing and promoting the civil and political rights of Persons with impairments. The legal framework, inclusive legislation, and awareness campaigns demonstrate the country's commitment to inclusivity. However, challenges such as physical inaccessibility and financial constraints need to be addressed to ensure the full and equal political participation of persons with disabilities in Cameroon. The government, in collaboration with civil society organizations, has undertaken awareness campaigns to promote the political rights of persons with disabilities. These campaigns aim to sensitize both the general public and political stakeholders about the importance of inclusive political participation. Efforts are being made to eliminate societal stereotypes and prejudices against PWIs, ensuring their equal access to the political process.

Despite the progress made, challenges persist in the realization of political rights for persons with impairments in Cameroon. Barriers such as physical inaccessibility, lack of sign language interpretation, and limited financial resources hinder the full participation of PWDs in political activities. There is a need for continued investment in infrastructure, capacity- building programs, and accessible technologies to address these challenges effectively.

Furthermore, greater emphasis should be placed on strengthening the enforcement of existing legislation and ensuring its effective implementation at all levels. This includes training electoral officials on disability rights and providing support to political parties to create an inclusive environment for PWIs.

The CRPD clearly states that all States must guarantee persons with disabilities their political rights, create the opportunities for them to exercise this right on an equal basis with others, and ensure that persons with impairments are able to fully participate in political and public life, for example through being able to vote and be elected. This involves ensuring that voting procedures, facilities and materials are appropriate, accessible and easy to understand and use by persons with disabilities. Persons with disabilities, together with others, have an equal responsibility for ensuring that they are able to exercise their political rights. This can be achieved through, amongst others, advocating for their rights, creating public awareness thereon and directly participating in public life.

CHAPTER FIVE

THE PROTECTIVE MECHANISMS FOR THE PROTECTION OF THE RIGHTS OF PERSONS WITH IMPAIRMENTS IN CAMEROON

5.0 Introduction

There are a number of problems plaguing persons with impairments throughout the world, such as discrimination, violation and abuse. The Human Rights treaty bodies rank the such persons as a vulnerable group, who are more susceptible to various forms of discrimination. While many documents and treaties refer to rights that have particular significance to persons with disabilities, Cameroon has enacted a comprehensive national instrument that thoroughly attends to the specific needs of and required protections for the rights of persons with disabilities. This is not to say that international instruments do not cover persons with impairments.[273] Many instruments exist that recognize specific rights of all persons, thereby clearly applying to them. These instruments range from international covenants to regional laws and regulations. However, even with all of the international

---

273 Ibid.

and regional legal instruments that exist, persons with impairments are still without a treaty tailored to their particular needs. As a result, the rights of the elderly are often ignored or even denied, indicating that the existing international legal framework falls short of ensuring their human rights. One way to better address their needs and ensure their rights and protection is to create a legally binding body by which governments are held accountable for the treatment of persons with disabilities. This chapter sets out to examine the various legal protective measures towards a human right- based approach on the rights of persons with impairments in Cameroon in the different sectors in the society.

5.2 Legislative Protective Mechanisms

There exists a plethora of laws for the protection of the rights of persons with impairments in Cameroon. These laws encompass international and regional ratified conventions, and domestic legal instruments. An analysis of these laws will help provide a better grasp of the legal framework at the national levels. Also, the government and NGOs have engaged several initiatives for the protection and promotion of the rights of PWDs in Cameroon.

5.2.1 The National Measures

At the Domestic level, there exist a plethora of laws for the protection of the rights of PWD's. which will be discussed below.

The Cameroonian Constitution,[274] the highest law of the Land, provides in its preamble that "the state shall provide all its citizens with conditions necessary for their development; the state shall ensure the protection of minorities and shall preserve the rights of indigenous populations in accordance with the law". The Preamble of the Cameroonian Constitution, therefore, obliges the state to ensure the protection of minorities. Worth mentioning is the fact that PWD's generally fall under the category of minorities, and hence their protection.

In order to comply with its commitments on the right to education, the government makes certain that the Constitution includes an explicit provision on the right to education for everyone.

---

274 Law No 96/06 of the 18th of January 1996 relating to the Constitution of Cameroon.

As a result, the Constitution states:

> "The State shall guarantee the child's right to education. Primary education shall be compulsory. The organisation and supervision of education at all levels shall be the bounden duty of the State."[275]

In order to carry out this provision, the government established a nursery and primary education system comprised of two and six grades of compulsory schooling respectively; a secondary education system comprising of general, and technical and commercial studies of seven years (five years for secondary school and two years for high school); and a higher education system which involves professional and academic programs of different fields of study. Furthermore, it designates distinct ministries as opposed to the former setting which was the Ministry of Education, to oversee basic education (nursery and primary schools), secondary and higher educations.

Most notably, in accordance with the World Conference on EFA"s conclusion in Jomtien, Thailand in 1990, the government adopted the Sector Plan for Primary Education, which is incorporated in Cameroon's 1998 Education Framework. This Plan was supplemented by the 2000 Dakar Framework for Action promoting EFA, which aimed to secure the availability of free primary education for all. As a result, it might be argued that the Cameroonian Constitution and the National Sector Plan for Primary Education are non- discriminatory, ensuring the inclusion of PWDs in primary schools. This is because the Constitution protects the right to equality and the right not to be discriminated against. The right to equality and the prohibition on discrimination apply to all areas, including education. As a result, everyone, boys and girls, should have equal access to education and should not face discrimination on any basis, including disability.

Nonetheless, as stipulated by the Constitution education shall be the bounden obligation of the State. In other words, the state has a moral (rather than a legal) commitment to respect the right to education. This means that the state is not only required to provide the right to education, but it is also required to ensure that the right is not hampered.

---

275 See para. 26 of the 1996 Constitution.

5.2.1.1 Inclusive Education in Technical and Vocational Education

The 2010 Law relating to the Protection and Welfare of Persons with Disabilities is the main law that protects the welfare of PWI's in Cameroon. In this respect, it aims at the prevention of disabilities; social, economic and psychological rehabilitation and integration of PWD's; and promotion of national solidarity in favour of PWI's. The law defines disability as a limitation of a person's ability, due to deficiency, to fully participate in an activity in a given environment. It highlights the various kinds of disabilities, to wit; physical, mental, and multiple disabilities.

The law provides various mechanisms for the prevention of disabilities and goes further to provide psychological support for PWI's.[276] This psychological support shall aim at strengthening psychological capacity, developing self-esteem, and strengthen relations with the living environment to reconcile PWD's with themselves and with their environment.[277] The law further guarantees the right to special education for PWD's,[278] socio-economic integration,[279] access to education and vocational training,[280] access to information and participation in cultural activities,[281] access to infrastructure, housing and transport,[282] participation in sport and leisure activities[283] and access to employment.[284] The law further provides for the issuance of a national disability card for PWD's which will permit them to enjoy these rights wherever they find themselves.[285]

The State shall compensate for the financial costs of education, vocational training, medical costs, disability allowance, housing assistance, support for the creation of work of art, construction of equipment or infrastructure, for rehabilitation and functional therapy, support for the equipping of work stations and other activities falling under national solidarity for PWD's.[286]

---

276 See Chapter II, articles 6-15 of the 2010 Law Relating to the Protection and Welfare of Persons with Disabilities.

277 *Ibid*, Arts. 16 -19.

278 *Ibid*, Arts. 24 - 26.

279 *Ibid*, Art. 27.

280 *Ibid*, Arts. 28 – 31.

281 *Ibid* Art. 32.

282 *Ibid*, Arts. 33 – 35.

283 *Ibid*, Arts. 36 & 37.

284 *Ibid*, Arts. 38 – 40.

285 *Ibid*, Art. 41.

286 *Ibid*, Art. 42.

The 2010 Law on the protection and promotion of PWIs remained in the shadows being unable to be applied for over eight years. However, following Decree No. 2018/6233/PM of 26th July 2018,[287] the law on the protection and promotion of the welfare of PWDs became applicable. This Decree of application in its chapter two, makes provision for the promotion and guarantee of the rights of PWDs to education in primary and secondary schools as well as universities. This Decree provides that, depending on the nature or degree of disability, education and vocational training for PWDs are provided either in standard training institutions and centers or in specialized training centers founded or sponsored by the state. Disability is in no way a justification for denying a student admission or registration in a traditional institution or training facility.[288]

The state has the prerogative to ensure the education of PWDs in traditional or special institutions. To do this, the state makes provision for certain needs that enhance the promotion of education for PWDs such as improving on communication methods to allow PWDs attend normal schools, improve school infrastructure to meet PWDs' needs, provision of specialized teachers as well as trainers in schools and universities amongst others. Remarkable in these measures is the substitution of the spell check exam for the dictation test for the hearing impaired.[289]

As a further step in the ensuring the guarantee of the rights of PWDs in official examinations, measures such as providing a special examination centers or rooms are providing for PWDs with special difficulties. Also, an extension of not more than one third of the normal time allowed for the examination is given to PWDs, etc.[290] More so, PWDs or children of PWDs are either partially or totally exempted from the payment of fees in schools and universities. They can also be granted scholarships as well as provided didactic materials relevant to their specific needs.[291]

This Decree of application further makes provision for the support of PWDs by strengthening the capacity of the teachers or lecturers involved with the students.[292] It goes further to make provision for a specialized tutor

[287] Decree No. 2018/6233/PM of 26th July 2018 Fixing the Procedures for the Application of Law N° 2010/002 Of 13 April 2010 on the Protection and Promotion of Persons with Disabilities in Cameroon.

[288] See Art. 3.

[289] See Art. 4.

[290] Art. 6.

[291] See the appendix of resolution 48/96.

[292] United Nations Department for Economic and Social Affairs, "Standard Rules on the Equalization

or supervisor, where necessary for the follow up of PWDs in schools and universities. In fact, the supervisor must have undergone training in the area of the disability of the supervisee.[293]

This however is just on paper as especially in universities most lecturers are not equipped in any way special to better handle the needs of PWDs. In fact, the PWDs are left to adapt on their with the rests of their mates. No added time in exams is often given for PWDs eve if they were late as a result of their disability either in time of entering the exams hall or in writing. Where some little time is added by examination personnel, they often make it seem like it was out of pity or just a favour not as of right of the PWDs.

In another respect, the Convention on Technical and Vocational Education[294] enshrines the "right of equal access to technical and vocational education". Article 1 defines technical and vocational education as: "all forms and levels of the educational process involving, in addition to general knowledge, the study of technologies and related sciences and the acquisition of practical skills, know-how, attitudes and understanding relating to occupations in the various sectors of economic and social life".

Key note is taken on article 2 which provides that states: "shall guarantee that no individual who has attained the educational level for admission into technical and vocational education shall be discriminated against" and "shall take appropriate measures" to enable people with disabilities and other marginalized groups to benefit from technical and vocational education. It further provides the basic content requirements as well as a list of elements to be taken into account when providing and developing technical and vocational education programs[295] as well as refers to teachers' training and employment conditions in the field of technical and vocational education, amongst other implementing provisions.[296] Again states are required to periodically review the structure of technical and vocational education[297] in order to meet the needs of everyone including PWDs.

---

of Opportunities for Persons with Disabilities" at https://www.un.org/development/desa/disabilities/standard-rules-on-the-equalization-of-opportunities-for-persons-with-disabilities.html (accessed on the 9th day of March 2023).

293 Rule 6 handles educational needs of PWDs.

294 Convention on Technical and Vocational Education (adopted 10 November 1989, entered into for 29 August 1991) 1649 UNTS 143.

295 UNESCO. 2019b. *The right to education.* The right to education handbook. UNESCO and Right to Education Initiative, p. 53 at http://creativecommons.org/licenses/by-sa/3.0/igo/ (accessed on 30th of Nov. 2022).

296 See Art. 28-30.

297 Art. 23.

The International Covenant on Economic, Social and Cultural Rights'(ICESCR) provisions on the right to education derive from both the socialist and liberal theoretical traditions, as the state's primary responsibility to provide educational services, and 2) as the state's duty to respect parents' rights to establish and direct private schools, as well as to ensure that their children receive an education that is consistent with their own religious and moral beliefs.[298] As a result, the ICESCR enumerates both negative and positive duties for states parties to offer education to their citizens. Despite these competing traditions shaping the right to education under the ICESCR, the aims and objectives of education have shifted toward a growing consensus in international human rights law that education should enable an individual to freely develop her own personality and dignity, participate in a free society, and respect human rights.[299]

Article 13 is the most comprehensive provision in the ICESCR on the right to education. It is also the most textually detailed clause in the ICESCR, demonstrating its significance and the broad normative scope of the right to education.

Furthermore, though there is no explicit mention of PWDs in the guarantee of the right to education, article 2 (2) of the ICESCR assures non-discrimination in the application of the treaty's human rights provisions. This means that Article 13 read in conjunction with Article 2 (2) imposes obligations on States parties to ensure the right to an education free of discrimination.

The UNESCO Convention against Discrimination in Education (1960), which has been acknowledged as a cornerstone of the Education 2030 Agenda, is the first legally enforceable international convention that lays out essential elements of the right to education. This convention bans all forms of discrimination in the sphere of education and affirms the idea of equal educational opportunity. Article 1(a) of the Convention states that denying any person or group of persons access to education of any kind or level constitutes discrimination.[300] The definition of "discrimination" in the article does not explicitly mention discrimination based on "disability". However, the list is non-exhaustive, and the Convention reflects the constitutional

---

298 Sital Kalantry, Jocelyn E. Getgen & Steven A. Koh,. (2010). "Enhancing Enforcement of Economic, Social and Cultural Rights Using Indicators: A Focus on the Right to Education in the ICESCR". *Human Rights Quarterly*, Vol. 32, p. 262.

299 Universal Declaration of Human Rights (adopted 10 December 1948) UNGA Res 217 A(III) (UDHR).

300 Ibid, p. 4.

mandate of UNESCO to ensure "full and equal opportunities for education for all" and aims at guaranteeing the right to education for all, particularly for marginalized and vulnerable groups, including people with disabilities.

Furthermore, Article 4 legally binds States Parties to create, develop, and implement a national policy that will tend to promote equality of opportunity and treatment in the field of education by methods adequate to the circumstances and to national usage. These provisions account for the national expansion of the right to education for all by encouraging States Parties to make their respective education systems more inclusive by providing equal access to education at all levels, particularly for the most disadvantaged groups.

Furthermore, UNESCO has adopted a number of other international standard-setting instruments, including one convention and seven recommendations that expand on various aspects of the right to education. Also, while the future UNESCO Global Convention on the Recognition of Higher Education Qualifications has not yet been adopted, the preamble states that Parties to the Convention are mindful of the UNESCO Convention against Discrimination in Education of 1960, Article 4a committing Member States to "make higher education equally accessible to all" and are "Reaffirming their responsibility to promote inclusive education, equitable quality of higher education, and lifelong learning."

5.2.1.2 Employment Measures relating to Workers with Impairments

The ILO, founded in 1919, is the oldest of the specialised technical agencies of the UN system. It is tripartite in structure, with representatives of employers' and workers' organizations[301] having an equal voice with those of governments of its 181 member States[302] in shaping ILO policies and programs, through participation in the annual International Labour Conference (ILC) and membership on the ILO Governing Body. The primary goal of the ILO is to promote opportunities for women and men to obtain decent and productive work, in conditions of freedom, equity, security and human dignity.[303]

Just a few years after the ILO was founded, the ILC adopted the first international document with rules relevant to the vocational rehabilitation of

---

301 Developmentaid.org (accessed on the 16th of August 2023).

302 Cameroon is the 74th member State of the ILO since 07th of June 1960.

303 Arthur O"Reilly (2007). *Op.cit.* p. 15.

workers with disabilities in 1925. The Workmen's Compensation (Minimum Scale) Recommendation, 1925 (No. 22), which outlined considerations for making compensation payments for industrial accidents, spelled out the principles to be used. Additionally, it urged governments to support organizations that would offer this "re-education" and advised that "the vocational re-education of injured workmen should be provided by such means as the national laws or regulations deem most suitable."[304]

Interest in vocational rehabilitation and employment opportunities for persons with disabilities re surfaced during the Second World War, largely because of the number of people disabled during the war and the need to find trained workers to fill jobs left vacant by mobilized workers.[305] The International Labor Conference (ILC) adopted Recommendation No. 71 in May 1944, which addressed the organization of full employment during the period of transition from war to peace and thereafter. This recommendation placed special emphasis on the employment services sector, including labor market data, career counseling, and vocational training. Disabled workers were one of the groups that the recommendation particularly addressed. The recommendation stated that persons with disability "should be provided with full opportunities for rehabilitation, specialized vocational guidance, training and retraining, and employment on useful work, whatever the origin of their disability."[306]

Although Recommendation No. 71 did not specifically refer to gender differences in the provisions concerning workers with disabilities, it did emphasize more than once "complete equality of opportunity" for men and women in respect, for example, of recruitment on the basis of their individual merit, skill and experiencc, equal pay for equal work, and access to further education and training.

The ILO's Conventions and Recommendations continue to be woven together by the organization's particular concern for employees with disabilities. The Medical Examination of Young Persons (Industry) Convention, 1946 (No. 77); Medical Examination of Young Persons (Non-Industrial Occupations) Convention, 1946 (No. 78); and Medical Examination of Young Persons Recommendation, 1946 (No. 79) concerning medical examination of young people for fitness for employment, required the competent authority to take

---

304 Arthur O"Reilly (2007). *Op.cit.* p. 15.

305 *Ibid.*

306 See para. 39 to 44 of The International Labor Conference (ILC) Recommendation No. 71.

appropriate steps for vocational guidance and vocational rehabilitation in regard to young people.[307]

When it came to the organization of employment services, the 1948 Employment Service Convention (No. 88) and Recommendation (No. 83) called for "conditions or special studies" on issues like the placement of disabled workers and called for special measures to meet their needs. A proposal that employment services not itself discriminate against job candidates based on their race, color, sex, or religious beliefs was also included.

5.2.1.3 Rights of Mentally Retarded Persons

Mental illness is a general term for a group of illnesses that affect the mind or brain. These illnesses, which include bipolar disorder, depression, schizophrenia, anxiety and personality disorders, affect the way a person thinks, feels and acts. A person with a mental health condition may experience difficulty concentrating, which can sometimes be a result of medication. Try to avoid overly stressful situations wherever possible so that their condition is not exacerbated.

A Declaration on the Rights of Mentally Retarded Persons was adopted by the UN General Assembly in 1971. The Declaration of Independence recognised that people with mental disabilities have the same rights as everyone else. They specifically had a right to the kind of education, training, rehabilitation, and guidance that would allow them to reach their full potential, as well as a right to financial security and a decent standard of living, as well as a right to engage in meaningful work to the best of their abilities.

5.2.1.4 Protective Measures under the Penal Code

In conformity with the provisions of the Cameroon Penal Code, the 2010 Law *inter alia* provides sanctions for individuals who violate the rules protecting the rights of persons with impairments in Cameroon. Pursuant to sections 45 of the law, officials of schools, vocational and University institutions, employers, corporate managers, guilty of discriminating in the admission, recruitment or pay of PWD's shall be punished with imprisonment for from 3 (three) to 6 (six) months and fine of from 100000 (one hundred thousand) to 1000000 (one million) CFA Francs. Sections 46 corroborates by

307 Arthur O"Reilly (2007). *Op.cit.* p. 18.

providing that, "whoever refuses to provide a service due to a person with a disability in accordance with this law and its enabling instruments shall be punished with the penalties outlined in sections 242 of the Cameroonian Penal Code.

5.1.1.5 Provision for Means of Transportation

A lack of accessible transportation is a significant barrier in accessing healthcare services, education and work for PWIs.[308] Railway networks are not accessible to wheelchair users,[309] little or no assistance is provided to assist passengers in accessing and using the different means of transportation,[310] and disabled passengers feel vulnerable because of safety concerns.[311] In addition, there are no telecoil (TTY) facilities available for passengers using hearing aids, and many transport agencies and the train stations have poor signage and unclear or no loudspeaker systems. The informal minibus taxi industry is of the main provider of public transport in Cameroon for both interurban and intraurban (especially in towns like Douala and Yaounde) transportation because of its availability and affordability. However, people with disabilities experience many challenges, including lack of assistance getting into and out of a taxi, being required to lift and carry their own wheelchairs on board, being charged an extra fare for their wheelchairs and concerns surrounding safety as well as even being denied to be carried by drivers for flimsy reasons.

Furthermore, the poor nature of road network in the country is a serious hinderance to many PWDs. For those attending school or who are employed the bad state of roads seriously affect their punctuality and sometimes presence in school or at work. For those suffering from physical disabilities such as amputees and the blind, movement from and to home is often difficult.

---

308 Sherry K. (2014). "Disability and rehabilitation: Essential considerations for equitable, accessible and poverty-reducing health care in South Africa". *South African Health Review Vol. 1*, pp. 89–99, at htt://www. hst.org.za/publications/southafrican-health-review-201415 (accessed on the 31st of March 2023).

309 In fact most of the railways which were important in transportation of persons and goods such as the Kumba- Mbanga-Douala railway, no longer function for several reasons unknown to the public.

310 Victor McKinney, Leslie Swartz & Emma L. McKinney, (2020). "COVID-19, disability and the context of healthcare triage in South Africa: Notes in a time of pandemic". *African Journal of Disability, Vol. 1;9(1)*, pp. 1–9. https://doi.org/10.4102/ajod.v9i0.766 (accessed on the 31st of March 2023).

311 Grut L. *et al.* (2012). "Accessing community health services: Challenges faced by poor people with disabilities in a rural community in South Africa". *African Journal of Disability, Vol. 1(1)*, p. 19. https://doi.org/10.4102/ajod.v1i1.19 (accessed on the 31st of March 2023).

Many potholes on main roads, the lack of pedestrian paths when roads are constructed etc. Imagine the difficulty persons without disabilities go through especially during the raining season to find themselves in school or work for example, jumping one stagnant water on main roads to another or creating bush pathways in order to avoid mud or stagnant water, then one will not know how PWDs manage to step out themselves.

5.1.1.6 The Protection of the Rights of All Migrant Workers and Members of Their Families

The International Convention on the Rights of All Migrant Workers and Members of Their Families.[312] aims to prevent and eliminate migrant worker exploitation throughout the migration process by establishing binding international standards for the treatment, welfare, and human rights of both documented and undocumented migrants, as well as the obligations and responsibilities of sending and receiving states.

Following articles 12 (4), 30, 43, and 45, the ICRMW guarantees for each child of a migrant worker the basic right of access to education on the basis of equality of treatment with nationals of the state even in cases of irregular migrant situations. It provides other rules for migrants and their families, in the field of education, and assures parental freedom in the moral and religious education of their children.

5.2.2 International Legislative Instruments on Persons with Impairments

This part of this work reviews, the principal international legal instruments concerned with the rights of persons with disabilities and especially those of the International Labour Organisation (ILO) and United Nations (UN).

5.2.2.1 The Convention on the Rights of Persons with Disabilities

The Convention on the Rights of Persons with Disabilities (CRPD) is one of the foremost international legal instruments that guarantee the rights

[312] International Convention on the Protection of the Rights of All Migrant Workers and Members of Their Families (adopted 18 December 1990, entered into force 1 July 2003) 2220 UNTS 3 (ICRMW).

of PWDs to education. This convention was adopted by the United Nations in 2006 and has been ratified by over 170 countries. The CRPD outlines the right of PWDs to access inclusive and quality education on the basis of non-discrimination and equality. It promotes the idea of mainstreaming PWDs into the education system, and requires states to provide reasonable accommodations for PWDs to access their education.

5.2.2.2 The Salamanca Declaration of 1994

The Salamanca Statement and Framework for Action on Special Needs Education is another international legal instrument that guarantees the rights of PWDs to education. This document, which was adopted by the World Conference on Special Needs Education in 1994, promotes the idea that all children, regardless of their disability, should have access to quality education. It outlines the need for inclusive education, where PWDs and non-PWDs learn together, as well as the importance of providing reasonable accommodations and support services to PWDs to ensure they can access and benefit from their education.

5.2.2.3 The Convention on the Elimination of All Forms of Discrimination against Women

The Convention on the Elimination of All Forms of Discrimination against Women (CEDAW) is also an international legal instrument that guarantees the rights of PWDs to education. This convention, which was adopted by the United Nations in 1979, requires states to take specific measures to ensure that PWDs, especially women and girls, have access to education on the basis of non-discrimination and equality. This includes providing reasonable accommodations and support services, as well as ensuring equality.

It is therefore of prime importance to discuss the above-mentioned legal instruments and others in a more expressive manner on their role in ensuring the promotion of the rights to education of PWDs in Cameroon.

5.3 Institutional Protective Measures for the Protection of the Rights of Persons with Impairments in Cameroon

After discussing the legal framework for the protection of the rights of PWD"s in Cameroon, it becomes necessary to ascertain the role played by institutional mechanisms in protecting these rights. Understanding how institutions embed, monitor, facilitate and implement the rights of PWD"s becomes important.

5.3.1 The Ministry of Social Affairs

The major ministry in charge of promoting the rights of PWIs is the Cameroonian Ministry of Social Affairs. Several Departments make up the Ministry. One of its core departments, the Social Protection of PWDs Department, is in charge of developing, carrying out, and overseeing PWDs' socioeconomic reinsertion policies as well as the government's special education, health assistance, equipment, and professional training policies. It also promotes development programs and the capacity to mobilize and manage resources of target populations, enters technical relationships with national and international organizations of promotion of PWDs, and collects statistical data on target populations in collaboration with the technical structures concerned. These actions further assist PWIs.

The Ministry has hitherto implemented various schemes for the betterment of PWI's. In 2006, the Ministry of Social Affairs took the following steps for the betterment of the rights of PWIs.[313]

On the 22nd of March 2006, the Minister of Social Affairs and the Director of National Social Insurance Fund (NSIF) signed an agreement aimed at improving assistance to PWis and victims of industrial accidents. The agreement was also implemented within NSIF, which provided its disabled staff members with special vehicles to facilitate their transport to work;

On 4 September 2006, a partnership agreement was signed between the Minister of Social Affairs and the National Director of National Employment Fund on facilitating the integration of vulnerable persons into training programs and gainful employment to help PWD's to economic and social independence;

A meeting between the Ministers of Higher Education and Social Affairs on 13 March 2006 led to the signature of a joint circular letter aimed at ameliorating the conditions of disabled and vulnerable students by providing

---

313 Awa M. Rumarick. "The Protection Of The Rights Of Persons With Disabilities (Pwd"s) In Cameroon: Prospects And Challenges." Human Rights And Legal Research Centre, 2021. At https://hrlrc.org/2021/06/17/the-protection-of-the-rights-of-persons-with-disabilities-pwds-in-cameroon-prospects-and-challenges/#:~:text=On%2022%20March%202006%2C%20the,and%-20victims%20of%20industrial%20acciden ts. (accessed on the 29th day of August 2023).

them with accommodations, integrating them into University "work-study programs" and finding vacation internships for them.

On 10 April 2006, a meeting was held between the Ministers of Social Affairs and Public Works to ensure the effective application of the 1983 Act on disabled persons' access to public buildings and of the related implementation Decree No. 90/1516 of 26 November 1990;

All these efforts mentioned hitherto have contributed immensely to the protection of the rights of PWIs in Cameroon.

5.3.2 The National Rehabilitation Centre for People with Disabilities (NRCPD)

The National Rehabilitation Center for People with Disabilities (NRCPD) is an additional agency in Cameroon that defends the rights of PWDs. The NRCPD was established by Cardinal Paul Emile LEGER in 1971, inaugurated on January 15, 1972, by His Excellency Hamadou Ahidjo, then President of the Federal Republic of Cameroon, and then passed to the State of Cameroon as a specialized Agency of the Ministry of Social Affairs.[314] The NRCPD"s mission is outlined in Decree No. 2009/096 of March 16, 2009, and it includes, among other things, the responsibility to carry out government policy on the rehabilitation and reconversion of people with disabilities, to provide psychological care for people with disabilities and their families, medical-social care for people with disabilities, training for people with disabilities, and socio-professional conversion of people with disabilities. All individuals with disabilities as well as their families are the focus of the CNRPH. This encompasses, among others, physically disabled individuals, individuals with sensory impairments, individuals with mental impairments, outcasts, and families of PWIs.

5.3.3 The National Commission on Human Rights and Freedoms (NCHRF)

The National Commission on Human Rights and Freedoms (NCHRF) is the main organization responsible for promoting and defending human rights and freedoms in Cameroon. The NCHRF is an autonomous organization that provides human rights promotion, protection, collective action, monitoring,

314 *Ibid.*

and assessment. Presidential Decree No. 90-1459 established the Commission first, followed by Law No. 2004/016, which was passed on November 8, 2004. The Comission's responsibilities include receiving complaints of human rights abuses, investigating and inspecting prison facilities, popularising human rights legislation, cooperating with NGOs, and recommending human rights-related legislation to the government. The NCHRF has the advantageous quality of offering free assistance for all human rights-related matters. As a result, PWIs whose rights have been violated can arrive at the commission's door without spending a single franc and receive justice for their suffering.

5.4 Conclusion

From the above overview of the various legislations protecting the rights of PWD"s at international, regional and national levels, there is no doubt that the quest for the protection of the rights of PWD"s is gaining ground everywhere around the globe. Albeit the fact that most of the laws are inspired very much from the Universal Declaration of Human Rights, they all share a similarity in that they apply to PWD's throughout the globe which renders their application much wider and beyond just a particular country or region.

However, PWDs are disadvantaged compared to their peers without disabilities as far as their access to decent work opportunities is concerned. This is partly attributed to limited formal education and skills. Persons with disabilities as a result tend to have worse labour market outcomes unemployment, partial employment or full employment at lower wages than persons without disabilities. Persons with disabilities can and should be active players in building the economy, and must therefore be enabled to access opportunities aimed at ownership of the economy.

A strategy to have a comprehensive legal instrument on the rights of persons with disabilities exist at the international level in both universal and regional systems. There are very few provisions in international law that directly address their rights. There are isolated efforts by certain international bodies to systematically refer to the rights of persons with disabilities when interpreting their corresponding conventions. Some declarations and other isolated statements by international fora have tried to fill this vacuum. However, there is no specific international body with the mandate to focus on the rights of persons with disabilities. Notwithstanding, a great effort and awareness in the recent years have been put in place to enhance these rights.

CHAPTER SIX

GENERAL CONCLUSION

6.1 Summary

Despite existing national, regional and international laws and other instruments, and despite the activities of international bodies and the efforts of NGOs, persons with disabilities throughout the world and Cameroon in particular continue to be subjected to widespread violations of their human rights. This is an undeniable fact in most sectors such as employment, education and even socialization. This is not to suggest that there has been no improvement. The significant growth in domestic anti-discrimination legislation in recent years is encouraging, even though adoption of a law does not guarantee its enforcement. The persistent efforts of international organs and instruments/policies, such as the ILO, in promoting equal opportunity and treatment in employment continue to make important inroads into the economic and social exclusion of persons with disabilities. It is hoped that the new era of adoption of legal instruments in relation to disability rights will reinforce national and international efforts and provide a renewed impetus in eliminating discrimination on the basis of disability and in positively promoting inclusion.

The CRPD and its accompanying Optional Protocol represent an extremely important effort to provide consistent, fundamental protections for persons with disabilities. The CRPD consists of 50 articles relating to the rights and treatment of persons with disabilities, and the Optional Protocol contains an additional 18 articles that allow persons with disabilities to vindicate their rights through the UN Committee on the Rights of Persons with Disabilities.

The CRPD and the Optional Protocol truly are human rights documents.[315] In its very first Article the Convention declares that, "the purpose of the present Convention is to promote, protect and ensure the full and equal enjoyment of all human rights and fundamental freedoms by all persons with disabilities, and to promote respect for their inherent dignity. The Convention is quite ambitious, attempting to address most aspects of civilized life, including, among other topics, accessibility, awareness raising, discrimination, liberty and security of person, independent living, personal mobility, education, employment, and recreation.[316]

The CRPD does not seek to establish new rights, but restates, reinforces and updates rights contained in other international instruments; confirms that all such rights apply to persons with disabilities; provides for the establishment of a Committee on the Rights of Persons with Disabilities to monitor the Convention; and obliges States Parties to closely consult with and actively involve persons with disabilities, through their representative organisations, in the development and implementation of legislation and policies to implement the Convention, and in other decision-making processes concerning issues relating to PWDs.

All of the CRPD's Articles are founded on the fundamental idea of defending and advancing the human rights of people with disabilities. Notably, Article 4 unambiguously binds States Parties to protect all people from human rights violations and to ensure and promote the full realisation of all human rights and fundamental freedoms for all people with disabilities, without any form of discrimination.

Additionally, the respect for, promotion, preservation, and fulfillment of all human rights are the cornerstones of the Cameroonian Constitution. The Government, Legislature, and Judiciary are the three branches of the State, and the Constitution requires them to carry out their respective constitutionally mandated duties in a manner that practically advances the realisation of these rights.

The Constitution requires the State to respect, protect, promote and fulfil the rights in the preamble. The state thus has the primary responsibility to guarantee the existence of circumstances in which every individual and community can exercise their rights. In this regard, the Government of Cameroon has passed a number of laws to give effect to its constitutional

315 David A. Larson. (2014). *Op.cit.* p. 225.

316 Ibid.

goals of achieving equality, human dignity and the advancement of human rights and freedoms amongst which are two disability laws with decrees of application.[317] The preamble of the Constitution, guarantees the right to equality to all, and prohibits discrimination on the grounds of, among others, disability. The constitution also recognises the use of all ratified international laws as part of the domestic laws of Cameroon.[318]

PWDs are among the most vulnerable and disadvantaged people in developing nations, with 82 percent of them living below the poverty line, according to UN figures. An estimated 20 percent of persons worldwide who subsist on less than $1 US (that is, about 600fcfa) are people with disabilities.[319] Their chances of escaping poverty are frequently hindered by a lack of enabling legislation to support their access to skill-development opportunities and employment opportunities (including life skills, technical skills, and entrepreneurship skills), as well as by lax implementation and enforcement measures where such legislation is present. People with disabilities who are living with HIV/AIDS are frequently ignored in policy and program initiatives, and women with impairments have greater difficulties earning a living than their male counterparts or non-disabled women.[320]

Persons with disabilities experience a number of interrelated challenges in accessing their rights, which include the following:

- Social barriers such as lack of awareness on the different types of disabilities amongst society, which results in lack of acceptance of persons with disabilities within communities; negative attitudes resulting from ignorance, misunderstanding and prejudice which keeps society from appreciating and experiencing the full potential PWDs can achieve.
- Psychological barriers which are mainly informed by fears for their personal safety.
- Structural barriers such as accessibility to facilities and infrastructure, the lack of support services or technology, the lack of availability of information in accessible formats and the lack of reasonable accommodation in schools and work places.

---

317 That is the 1983 Disability Law and its 1990 Decree of Application and the 2010 Disability law and its 2018 Decree of application.

318 See Section 64 of the 1996 Constitution.

319 UN Department of Economic and Social Affairs. Factsheet on Persons with Disabilities. At https://www.un.org/development/desa/disabilities/resources/factsheet-on-persons-with-disabilities.html (accessed on the 31st of August 2023).

320 Ibid.

6.2 Findings

The 2010 Law on Disability just like the CRPD supports PWD empowerment by addressing disability concerns in the framework of human rights and by connecting disability issues to economic, social, civil, political, and cultural rights. It is founded on the beliefs that people with disabilities have the right to equal opportunity, the right not to be discriminated against, and the right to fully and effectively participate in and be included in society.[321] It recognises that all persons are equal before and under the law and are entitled, without any discrimination, to the equal protection and equal benefits of the law.[322] It also calls for the prohibition of all discrimination on the basis of disability and the guarantee that PWDs be accorded equal and effective legal protection against discrimination.[323] It further requires that appropriate steps are taken to ensure that reasonable accommodation is provided so as to promote equality and eliminate discrimination.[324]

It sees the denial of reasonable accommodation as a form of discrimination on the basis of disability. It additionally advocates the empowerment of PWDs by calling for the elimination of all barriers to their living independently and participating fully in all aspects of life by ensuring their access, on an equal basis with others, to the physical environment, to transportation, to information and communications, including information and communication technologies and systems, and to other facilities and services open or provided to the public.[325]

However, regardless of the provisions of the CRPD, many PWDs are not afforded the opportunity to empower themselves. It has therefore become necessary for PWDs to be given the means to survive and take advantage of the opportunities which the twenty-fist century has to offer and empower themselves economically without discrimination.[326] As such, all barriers, be they financial, economic, political, social or psychological, which hinder PWDs from being accorded equal opportunities should be eliminated. This

---

321 Art. 3 of the CRPD.

322 Art. 5(1) of the CRPD.

323 Art. 5(2) of the CRPD.

324 Art. 5(3) of the CRPD.

325 Art. 9 of the CRPD.

326 Lex Frieden. (2003). "Perspectives on the status of people with disabilities internationally" at http://www.lexfrieden.com/_lfrieden/lfriedenperspectives0603.html (accessed on the 10th April 2023).

can be achieved through education, employment, vocational rehabilitation and the provision of financial resources/services.

With regard to work and employment, States Parties to the CRPD recognize the right of persons with disabilities to work, on an equal basis with others; this includes the right to the opportunity to gain a living by work freely chosen or accepted in a work environment that is open, inclusive and accessible. States Parties also undertake to take appropriate steps, including those specifically listed in the CRPD, to safeguard and promote the realization of the right to work.

There are numerous additional ways in which people with disabilities differ considerably from people without disabilities in terms of their ability to exercise socio-economic rights. First, infractions of a comparable type frequently affect people with disabilities differently from non-disabled people, especially those who have intellectual and psychosocial disabilities.[327] The psychological and physical effects that persons with intellectual disabilities experience as a result of breaches of their socio-economic rights and freedoms will usually be greater than those suffered by non-intellectually disabled persons due to their different level of mental development. This is certainly true with regard to the direct impact that breaches of the right to an adequate standard of living can have on an intellectually disabled person's psychological state.

Furthermore, PWDs who belong to other vulnerable groups are more exposed to breaches of their socio-economic rights and freedoms than persons with disabilities who do not belong to such groups.[328] All of this depends on their suffering from both the disadvantages and fragilities of their condition as persons with disabilities and those deriving from detention, non-citizenship, status as an indigenous person, gender, etc. For example, it is more likely that women with disabilities will experience socio-economic rights breaches more often than those living without a fact that derives from the particular exclusion experienced by such women.[329] It can be argued that persons with

---

[327] Monika Domańska, (2018). "People with Disabilities as a Vulnerable Group. The Concept of Protection of the Rights of Vulnerable Groups", *BialostockieI Studia Prawnicze Vol. 23*, No. 4, p. 28.

[328] Neta Ziv. (2007). "The Social Rights of People with Disabilities: Reconciling Care and Justice". In D. Barak-Erez & A.M. Gross (Eds.). *Exploring Social Rights: Between Theory and Practice*. London: Hart Publishing, p. 369, at http://dx.doi.org/10.5040/9781472564214.ch-015 (accessed on the 10th of April 2023).

[329] Rangita de Silva de Alwis. (2009). "Mining the Intersections: Advancing the Rights of Women and Children with Disabilities Within an Interrelated Web of Human Rights". *Pacific Rim Law &*

disabilities who suffer such multiple disadvantages are the victims of various discriminations at once.

In the past few years housing rights have become a major locus of activity in the field of economic and social human rights. The growing importance of this particular area of human rights is reflected not only in a rapidly increasing number of professional publications, studies, and reports dealing with this subject, but primarily in significantly more distinct actions undertaken by international organizations and humanitarian institutions. Decisions made under the aegis of the United Nations system play a leading role in the protection of housing rights, especially in the form of discussions at the United Nations General Assembly, United Nations Economic and Social Council, Office of the High Commissioner for Human Rights, United Nations Housing Rights Program (UNHRP), and the United Nations Human Settlement Program (UN-HABITAT).[330]

Again, PWDs have substantial obstacles in obtaining healthcare treatments and support, particularly those who reside in low and middle-income countries. People with disabilities are more marginalised and excluded during disasters and emergencies. For instance, many people with disabilities were unable to access healthcare facilities, get therapeutic treatments or rehabilitation, or obtain medication during the coronavirus disease 2019 (COVID-19) pandemic. Among those who have access to facilities, many face difficulties and occasionally outright discrimination in receiving life-saving care like ventilator support and admittance to intensive care units.

PWDs may have specific health needs due to their disabilities and associated health conditions. Evidence indicates that people with disabilities have greater health needs than people without disabilities and that these needs are generally not met.[331] In addition to the common health needs, such as immunization, they have worse levels of access to health services and worse health outcomes, especially in low, income countries, such as Cameroon. This situation is indeed evident in our country, where studies indicate that people with disabilities show higher levels of morbidity, behaviors that have a negative impact on health, and greater use of health services and hospitalizations.

Policy Journal Vol. 18, p. 293.

330 Bogumil Terminski. (2011). "The Right to Adequate Housing in International Human Rights Law: Polish Transformation Experiences". *Revista Latinoamericana de Derechos Humanos Vol. 22* (2), p. 220.

331 Karina A.P. Clemente, Simone V. da Silva, Gislene I. Vieira. *et al.* (2022). "Barriers to the access of people with disabilities to health services: a scoping review". *Revista Saude Publica. Vol. 56:64*, p. 2 at https://doi.org/10.11606/s1518-8787.2022056003893 (accessed on the 31st of March 2023).

People with disabilities, therefore, need adequate general health care that covers all aspects, including prevention and health promotion, based on primary, secondary, and tertiary care, and may also require rehabilitation care and specialized treatment related or not to their underlying disability to "optimize functionality and reduce disability."[332]

Although fundamental for the performance of health systems worldwide, access to health care by people with and without disabilities remains a complex concept.[333] Potential challenges faced in accessing health care include discrimination, physical inaccessibility, information inaccessibility and unavailability. Around the world, evidence on how to promote the inclusion of people with disabilities in the health system is lacking.

Furthermore, the pervasiveness of ratification of human rights treaties also means that there can be a more comprehensive response to the negative impacts of globalisation on social security: States are able, or should be compelled, to refer to their international obligations when faced with unreasonable demands for structural adjustment, cuts in social security spending etc. Furthermore, many countries have incorporated the right to social security or the above human rights treaties in their national constitutions, which means the potential for national application of the right. A greater emphasis on the content on the right would help guide court decisions and policymaking. However, while national courts and other adjudicatory and political bodies will have the opportunity to monitor the right, it is difficult to conclude that the international enforcement mechanisms for the human rights treaties can rival the ILO system, both in terms of focus upon the respective contributions and the high-level participation of employee and employer groups, which increases the likelihood of implementation.[334]

Also, to all intents and purposes, however, it will only be by good coordination of the different levels that trade union action will be most effective. Trade union bodies could examine two additional topics. The first is the place and role of PWDs within the unions themselves. What are unions doing to enable PWDs to participate in trade union activities within and outside the enterprise? What is being done regarding accessibility of meeting

---

332 Ibid.

333 Levesque J.F., Harris M.F., & Russell G. (2013). "Patient-centred access to health care: conceptualizing access at the interface of health systems and populations". International Journal of Equity & Health. Vol. 12:18 at https://doi.org/10.1186/1475-9276-12-18 (accessed on the 31st of March 2023).

334 Malcolm Langford. (2007). *Op.cit*, p. 31.

rooms, means of communication allowing persons with sensory impairments to receive information and express their opinions on the action programs and directions being taken by their union, how their specific needs are being analysed and taken into account within trade union claims, at all levels of the organization. In other words, the issue before trade unions is that of full participation by people with disabilities in the democratic life of the enterprise on a basis of equality with all other employees and the ways and means deployed by the unions to make this full participation possible.

The objective of the law for PWDs is to ensure that persons with disabilities are entitled to exercise their civil, political, social, economic and cultural rights on an equal basis with others. The term "disability" includes a great number of different functional limitations occurring in any population in any country of the world. People may be disabled by physical, intellectual or sensory impairment, medical conditions or mental illness. Such impairments, conditions or illnesses may be permanent or transitory in nature."

The UN estimates that there are 500 million persons with disabilities in the world today. This number is increasing every year due to factors such as war and destruction, unhealthy living conditions, or the absence of knowledge about disability, its causes, prevention and treatment.

Among persons with disabilities, the following form particularly vulnerable groups that face discrimination based on two grounds: women, children, elders, victims of torture, refugees and displaced persons, and migrant workers. For instance, women with a disability are discriminated against because of their gender and also because of their disability.

Persons with disabilities suffer from discrimination based on society's prejudice and ignorance. In addition, they often do not enjoy the same opportunities as other people because of the lack of access to essential services.

International human rights law determines that every person has:

- The right of equality before law;
- The right to non-discrimination;
- The right to equal opportunity;
- The right to independent living;
- The right to full integration; and
- The right to security

Policy regarding disabilities is often dominated by the notion of "equalisation of opportunities", which means that society must employ its resources in such a way that every individual, including persons with disabilities, has an equal opportunity to participate in society.

The UN undertakes important decisions and actions in the area of disability. Based on the International Bill of Rights, the UN formulated the first specific document regarding disabilities in 1971 in the Declaration on the Rights of Mentally Retarded Persons. In 1981, the General Assembly declared the first International Year of Disabled Persons. It was followed by the World Program of Action Concerning Disabled Persons in 1982 and the Decade of Disabled Persons 1983-1992. Throughout the 1990s all UN conferences dealt with disability rights and addressed the need for protective instruments (World Conference on Human Rights 1993, Fourth World Conference on Women 1995, Habitat II 1996).

The following international instruments protect the rights of persons with disabilities. They mainly focus on protecting PWDs from discrimination and creating equal opportunities for them to participate in society:

- The Universal Declaration of Human Rights (UDHR)[335] which was adopted by the General Assembly of the United Nations in 1948 and provides human rights standards accepted by all member states. The UDHR represents the normative basis that led to formulating the standards concerning persons with disabilities that exist today. In Article 25 (1) the UDHR specifically mentions the socio-economic rights of people with disabilities: the right to an adequate standard of living, including food, clothing, housing and medical care and social services, and the right to security in the event of unemployment, sickness, disability, widowhood, old age. Article 7 guarantees equality before the law and equal protection by the law for all people, including against discrimination.
- International Covenant on Civil and Political Rights: This treaty lists several rights that are relevant to disability. Article 26 states that all people are equal before the law and have the right to equal protection of the law.
- International Covenant on Economic, Social and Cultural Rights: The Covenant does not explicitly refer to disability. However, disability can be included under "other status" in article 2 (2), which calls for non-discrimination on any grounds such as race and color, and "other status".

335 See Articles 3, 21, 23 and 25.

- Declaration on the Rights of Mentally Retarded Persons: This declaration was proclaimed by the UN General Assembly and provides that the mentally retarded person has, to the maximum degree of feasibility, the same rights as other human beings.

- Declaration on the Rights of Disabled Persons: This declaration adopted by the UN General Assembly is the first international document that tried to define the term "disability." The Declaration includes a number of social and economic rights as well as civil and political rights.

- Declaration on the Rights of Deaf-Blind Persons; Article 1 of the Declaration states that "...every deaf-blind person is entitled to enjoy the universal rights that are guaranteed to all people by the Universal Declaration of Human Rights and the rights provided for all disabled persons by the Declaration of the Rights of Disabled Persons."

- Convention on the Elimination of Discrimination Against Women: The Convention abbreviated as CEDAW, does not include any specific article on disability rights, but aims to protect the rights of all women, whether disabled or not. Disabled women face double discrimination based on their gender and secondly, on their disability. In General Recommendation 18 the Committee on the Elimination of Discrimination Against Women, the monitoring body of the CEDAW convention, stresses that disabled women suffer from double discrimination and are a particularly vulnerable group. It recommends that governments provide information on disabled women in their period reports and on special measures that governments have taken to ensure that women with disabilities "have equal access to education and employment, health services and social security, and to ensure that they can participate in all areas of social and cultural life."

- Convention (No. 159) concerning Vocational Rehabilitation and Employment (Disabled Persons) (1983): This treaty of the International Labour Organization (ILO), a UN specialized agency, obligates states to "formulate, implement and periodically review a national policy on vocational rehabilitation and employment of disabled persons."[336] This treaty also emphasizes the principle of equal opportunity: "positive measures aimed at effective equality of opportunity and treatment

[336] See Art. 2.

between disabled workers and other workers shall not be regarded as discriminating against other workers."[337]

- Convention on the Rights of the Child (1989): This treaty lists disability as one of the grounds for which discrimination is prohibited.[338] In addition, article 23 directly addresses the rights of children with disabilities stating that disabled children are entitled to a "full and decent life" of dignity and participation in the community.
- Standard Rules on the Equalization of Opportunities for Persons with Disabilities: Adopted by the General Assembly in 1993 in the aftermath of the Decade of Disabled Persons, the Standard Rules do not constitute a legally binding document for member states. However, the Standard Rules are the most comprehensive set of human rights standards regarding disability police to date and represent "a strong moral and political commitment of governments to take action to attain equalization of opportunities for persons with disabilities." The document addresses preconditions for equal participation, target areas of equal participation, implementation measures and monitoring mechanisms.
- Convention on the Rights of Persons with Disabilities: It entered into force in May 2008 and was recently ratified by Cameroon. It is the most comprehensive international law on PWDs and its provisions encompasses the civil, political, socio- economic and cultural rights of PWDs.

A major outcome of the International Year of Disabled Persons (1981) was the formulation of the World Program of Action Concerning Disabled Persons (WPA) (1982). The WPA is a global strategy to enhance disability prevention, rehabilitation and equalisation of opportunities, which pertains to full participation of persons with disabilities in social life and national development. The WPA also emphasises the need to approach disability from a human rights perspective.

Although IHL and the CRPD have different roots, they have a lot in common when it comes to recognizing the unique capacities, experiences, and perspectives of people with disabilities in armed conflict. This is especially evident in the evaluation of prohibited inhuman acts and the call

[337] Art. 4.

[338] See Art. 2.

for the adoption of specific positive measures for people with disabilities in order to enable their effective access to services on an equal footing with others. These actions could involve modifying infrastructure, providing information on essential services like water, food, shelter, health care, and rehabilitation, facilitating the transportation of food and non-food relief supplies, maintaining the provision of particular services needed by people with disabilities, or helping those who have been harmed by the use of particular weapons in armed conflicts. The fact that IHL puts obligations on organized non-state armed organizations in addition to State armed forces, as opposed to the CRPD, which only binds States party to it, explains why people with disabilities are given additional protection under IHL.

IHL may additionally prevent or reduce harm to people with disabilities brought on by particular hazards to them during armed conflict. The current efforts to operationalize enhanced inclusion and engagement of people with disabilities in humanitarian actions in armed conflict may be facilitated by understanding the complimentary and mutually reinforcing character of IHL and the CRPD.

Furthermore, it might be tempting to claim that Cameroon's initiatives and/or action plans for protecting the rights of people with disabilities have been effective in achieving significant advancements in human rights in the context of the fight for the protection of those rights. Such a business would have serious problems.

PWDs in Cameroon struggle to move from one location to another. Many of the roads are muddy and unpaved with series of potholes. The majority of the areas are mountainous, and the topography is hilly. This means that getting around on these terrains can be difficult for people with mobility issues.

Moreover, PWD's continue to face stigmatisation. Most parents who have children with disabilities don't send them to school. This is because they think that it's a wastage of money as they may not easily gain employment in the future.

Again, PWDs are among the most vulnerable and disenfranchised groups in any nation experiencing a crisis. A cycle of fatal violence has been raging in Anglophone districts since the Anglophone crisis began to pick up steam. For PWDs, the crisis has made an already challenging position worse as PWDs had been among those killed, brutally attacked, or abducted by armed separatists and government troops. The crisis in the Anglophone regions has exacerbated an already difficult situation for PWD's.

Several reasons could be advanced for the aforementioned challenges. They include *inter alia,* the lack of awareness of the existence of disability rights, weak enforcement of existing laws and policies, and the lack of a political will for their implementation. It is therefore imperative that policy formulation, legitimization, implementation, and evaluation be given credence in matters related to disabilities.

6.3 Recommendations

The recommendations herein will go a long way to encourage, educate and create more awareness of disability rights as well as improve on their promotion and protection within the society.

6.3.1 Improve on Infrastructures to suit PWDs

Although the 2010 law on the protection and promotion of the rights of PWDs provides for accessibility of buildings and transportation, much more has to be done to ensure accessibility of the built environment, particularly schools, for people with disabilities. There is a need to transform the entire society into one that is inclusive, which will have an impact on the educational system. Additionally, disability awareness should be included in the training of city planners, architects, and construction engineers. As a result, all buildings and public areas, including schools, will be universally accessible.

6.3.2 Improve on Education for PWDs

Multidisciplinary collaboration with many education stakeholders is required to improve the promotion of education for PWDs. In this regard, parents of PWDs and activists in the disability movement should collaborate to provide educational provision for PWDs. Similarly, there is a need to train and develop more teachers than there are currently available to meet the different requirements of learners. It is critical to incorporate curriculum development professionals in order to establish an inclusive education based on ULD that benefits all learners, including those with disabilities.

Again, the inclusion of PWDs in especially elementary schools necessitates a systemic shift, not just in teaching methodologies and institutions, but also in addressing cultural beliefs that obstruct inclusive education. To do this, parents must be educated on the need of enrolling their children with disabilities in school, as well as support them and engage directly with teachers to ensure full inclusion of these children in schools and society.

6.3.3 Recommendations to Improve Healthcare

The health status of persons with disabilities is often poorer than that of the general population. Until relatively recently such differences were frequently viewed as an inevitable consequence of disability, but it is increasingly recognised that they may actually be the result of inequalities and inequities in access to healthcare. Problems of disability are largely manifested in social contexts and social relations, rather than in an individual"s medical condition. In the context of health, stigma and prejudice give rise to additional barriers that are then faced by persons with disabilities. These include physical barriers that prevent access for persons with disabilities to health clinics and hospitals; informational barriers that prevent access for persons with disabilities to health literacy and information brochures and leaflets on health promotion, prevention and protection; attitudinal barriers which give rise to discrimination that can have severe implications for the rights of persons with disabilities, particularly for those with psychosocial disabilities; and institutional barriers that include legislation, practices and processes that prohibit access to health services for persons with disabilities. Services for people with physical, sensory or intellectual disabilities have also been the subject of criticism in relation to communication and cultural barriers.

Access to healthcare for persons with disabilities extends well beyond the accessibility factors described above. Differences in access to health and social services may arise due to availability insofar as services may be scarce or simply not be provided to certain groups, quality may vary between groups, and not all groups may be aware of certain services owing to information deficiencies. It is important both to enhance the capacity of persons with disabilities to access the healthcare system and also to ensure that the system is able to respond in an appropriate and timely manner to their needs.

Again, while ensuring that PWDs have access to general health services, some specialist services, such as rehabilitation services, may be needed. For example, in some cases persons require care or rehabilitation services specific to their impairment. Many countries have a National Rehabilitation Hospital or Centre just like Cameroon, which provides specialist services to patients from all over the country who, as a result of accident, illness or injury, have acquired a physical or cognitive disability and require specialist rehabilitation. The difficulty in many countries including Cameroon is that such facilities can only treat a limited number of patients, resulting in lengthy waiting periods or even denial of treatment. As such it is imperative that more of these centres are constructed in different parts of the country as traveling to the already existing few centres present another challenge. The state may offer subsidies or even offer grants to the private centres such as the Baptist Convention centre-Mbingo Annex in Bamenda to improve on its structures and equipments so as to accommodate more PWDs for treatment.

Also, States should take appropriate measures to ensure access for PWDs to health services that consider gender issues, including health-related rehabilitation. Therefore, actions must be committed by the states to favor the reduction in gaps in access to health for PWDs, contributing to greater equity since these people require more health care and, on the contrary, they find greater access restrictions. From this perspective, universal access constitutes a challenge for health systems, as it implies generating innovations to traditional actions, ensuring the necessary resources to provide efficient and sustainable care over time. In this sense, health systems should play an active role in providing timely and permanent care for all people.[339]

Again, while several countries have taken steps to establish disability-inclusive health services, some countries, especially developing countries including Cameroon still lack strategies to ensure adequate access to health services for PWDs, despite having a considerable burden to do so. Due to various socio-economic and cultural differences, the strategies of high-income countries may not be applicable in low-income countries such as Cameroon. The strategy for establishing disability friendly healthcare must therefore be country- and context-specific.

---

[339] Campillay-Campillay M. *et al.* (2022). "Accessibility in People with Disabilities in Primary Healthcare Centers: A Dimension of the Quality of Care". *International Journal of EnvironmentalResearch and Public Health*, *19*, 12439. https://doi.org/10.3390/ijerph191912439 (accessed on the 31st of March 2023).

6.3.4 Improve on Working Conditions of PWDs through Trade unions

The five key categories with respect to obtaining, keeping and returning to work include:

- The first is that of public policies and initiatives to be taken with a view to positively influencing their orientation. By intervening appropriately on their own behalf or as part of alliances with other players in the civil society, trade unions can oblige lawmakers to take account of the problems facing disabled workers and to amend then laws and regulations hampering their full participation.
- The second concerns programs of allowances and compensation implemented by countries. Depending on their level, their scope for combining work with allowance payments and how they are managed, these systems may achieve satisfactory occupational integration, or contrarily, may confine PWDs to activities that sideline them and which they can leave only at the risk of marginalisation.
- The third relates to rehabilitation and job assistance services. Here again, the orientation of these services will be all-important in determining whether they will promote inclusion in mainstream areas of vocational training or continue to restrict people with disabilities to a closed environment. In many countries, trade unions carry significant responsibility in the management of vocational training and it is for them, if they have the political will to do so, to further the cause of openness.
- The fourth category addresses the adaptation of jobs and workplaces. It is inconceivable that trade unions could have nothing to do or say in this connection when, as has been stated before, they are at the very core of the production process. Admittedly, the matter of determining what is reasonable adaptation of workplaces pursuant to anti-discrimination laws is a formidably complex one. But ever more frequent trade union use of ergonomic studies has enabled them to acquire expertise in this field that no one can seriously contest.
- The fifth and last category covers strategies implemented at enterprise level under what is known as "disability management". Sometimes falling within the framework of codes of good practices jointly worked out by

management and labour, these strategies simultaneously aim to meet the needs of enterprises stemming from their statutory obligations with respect to hiring and recruitment, and additionally to promote innovation by combining financial considerations (how the enterprise can minimize the costs entailed) with social goals of improved occupational health and safety and disability prevention.

6.3.5 According Attention to PWDs during and after Crisis and Emergencies

The needs of persons with a disability are shaped in light of the scope of their vulnerability and their specific situation as explained above. Their main needs, in terms of the armed conflict, can be stated as the needs, which occur during the warning, evacuation, humanitarian aid and planning and registration. Warnings should be made in a way that all people including persons who are deaf and the blind can understand. All evacuation and humanitarian aid activities should be planned while considering the need for accessibility. Additionally, PWDs should be registered properly in order to not be excluded from humanitarian aid.

Furthermore, peace agreements can include provisions on protection and humanitarian assistance during conflict. They can also seek to include and empower persons with disabilities politically, in terms of contributions to the peace process, in political institutions, and in terms of participation in democratic processes. In addition, peace agreements can also include provisions on socio-economic inclusion and empowerment.

6.3.6 Ensure Equal Access to Information and Communication Platforms

All electronic media, broadcasting and print media platforms of all public and private media institutions and agencies must incorporate universal design principles, meet minimum norms and standards regulatory requirements, and government agencies regulating them should publish annual compliance reports.

6.3.7 Develop and Regulate Braille Standards

A costed plan should be developed for the continuous development, production and regulation of braille standards. Adequate budget must be provided for implementation of the plan.

6.3.8 People with print difficulties should have access to print media

To guarantee that people with print disabilities have access to print, all necessary measures must be done. Ratifying the Marrakesh Treaty to Facilitate Access to Published Works for Persons Who Are Blind, Visually Impaired, or Otherwise Print Disabled should be one of the first stages.

6.3.9 Promote access for Persons with Disabilities to New Information and Communications Technologies and Systems

All public and private institutions should promote access to new information and communications technologies and systems, including the internet. This can be done through the design, development, production and distribution of accessible information and communications technologies and systems at an early stage, so that these technologies and systems become available at minimum cost.

6.3.10 Develop and Implement Universal Design Minimum Standards and Guidelines

This should be done by all public and private sector institutions. The institutions must also monitor implementation of the strategy, compliance with the minimum standards and utilisation of the guidelines. The standards and guidelines must include all facilities and services open or provided to the public, including those rendered by operators/contractors.

SELECTED BIBLIOGRAPHY

Books

John L. Holland. (1985). *Making vocational choices: A theory of vocational personalities and work environments (2nd ed.)*. Englewood Cliffs, NJ: Prentice-Hall.

Kanter S. Arlene. (2015). *The Development of Disability Rights Under International Law: From Charity to Human Rights*. New York, Routledge.

Leandro Depouy. 1993. *Human rights and Disabled Persons*. UN Center for Human Rights, New York.

Marianne Schulze. (2010*). Understanding the UN Convention on the Rights of Persons with Disabilities*. A Handbook on the Human Rights of Persons of Disabilities, 3rd edition, Paper Slam.

Patterson, C. H. (2021). *Services marketing: an Asia-Pacific and Australian perspective*. Latrobe.edu.au; Frenchs Forest, N.S.W: Pearson Education Australia.

Richard Bellamy. (2007). *Political constitutionalism: A Republican defense of constitutionality of democracy* Cambridge: Cambridge university Press.

Articles

Adam S. Chilton & Mila Versteeg. (2018). "Courts Limited Ability to Protect Constitutional Rights." *University of Chicago Law Review Vol. 85.*

Adam, M. S. (2007) "What Good Is the Social Model of Disability?",*74 University of Chicago Law Review*. Pages 1251-1308.

Anne, T. B. (2000), "Waking Sleeping Beauty: The Revised European Social Charter", *7 Human Rights Brief*, Issue 2, pages. 24-27.

Ardha, D. and Carol, W. (2005), "Emancipatory Research Methodology and Disability: A Critique", *8 International Journal of Social Research Methodology*, pages 281-96.

Agbor C. Nda. (2020). "The practice of social security in black Africa: a shadow of the real concept: The Cameroonian transcript". *International Journal for Innovation Education and Research Vol:-8 No-10*, at www.ijier.net (accessed on the 31st of March 2023).

Amita Dhanda. (2005). "The right to treatment of persons with psychosocial disabilities and the role of the courts." *International Journal of Law & Psychiatry, Vol. 28.*

Anna Lawson & Angharad E. Beckett. (2021). "The social and human rights models of disability: towards a complementarity thesis." *The International Journal of Human Rights, 25:2.*

Anna Lawson & Angharad E. Beckett. (2021). "The social and human rights models of disability: towards a complementarity thesis." *The International Journal of Human Rights, 25:2.*

Anwuli Irene Ofuani, (2011), "The right to economic empowerment of persons with disabilities in Nigeria: How enabled?" *African Human Rights Law Journal.*

Appelbaum S. Paul, (2016), "Protecting the Rights of Persons with Disabilities: An International Convention and Its Problems." *Psychiatric Services Vol 67 Issue 4*, at ps.psychiatryonline.org (accessed on the 20th of February 2022)

Arora R. "National programme for rehabilitation of persons with disabilities – A blend of CBR and IBR" at http://www.aifo.it/english/resources/online/apdrj/frimeet202/national.doc (accessed on the 12th of April 2023)

Arturs Kucs, Zane Sedlova& Liene Pierhurovica. "The Right to Housing: International, European and National Perspectives." *CuadernosConstitucionales de la Cátedra Fadrique FurióCeriol nº 64/65.*

Ashley Walker, *et al.* (2016). "When everything changes: Parent perspectives on the challenges of accessing care for a child with a disability". *Disability Health Journal* Vol. 9(1).

Azubike Onuora-Oguno. (2018). "Leaving the woods to see the trees: Locating and refocusing the activities of non-state actors towards the effective promotion of access to justice of persons with disability." In Charles Ngwena*et al.African Disability Rights Yearbook, Volume* 6, (eds) Pretoria University Law Press.

Beckman Paula J., *et al.*, 2016, "From rights to realities: Confronting the challenge of educating persons with disabilities in developing countries", *Global Education Review*, 3 (3).

Bhavisha Virendrakumar*et al.* (2018) Disability inclusive elections in Africa: a systematic review of published and unpublished literature, *Disability & Society, 33:4.*

Bill Dupes "Vocational rehabilitation: Helping people with disabilities in jobs and careers". at http://www.amputee-coalition.org/easyread/fist_step_2005/voc_rehabez.pdf (accessed on the 12th of April 2023).

Blasius A. Chiatoh, (2014), "Community language promotion in remote contexts: case study on Cameroon", *International Journal of Multilingualism*, 11:3.

Bogumil Terminski. (2011). "The Right to Adequate Housing in International Human Rights Law: Polish Transformation Experiences". *Revista Latino Americana de Derechos Humanos Vol. 22* (2).

Bolima S. Ambang. (2021). "The Right to Fair Trial as Guaranteed under the Cameroon Criminal Law System: A Critical Appraisal of the Cameroon Criminal Procedure Code". *Journal of Legal Studies and Research Volume 7 Issue 2.*

Bukala R. Akintola. (2010). "The right to inclusive education in Nigeria: Meeting the needs of and challenges of children with disabilities". *African Human Rights Law Journal.*

Campillay-Campillay M. *et al.* (2022). "Accessibility in People with Disabilities in Primary Healthcare Centers: A Dimension of the Quality of Care". *International Journal of EnvironmentalResearch and Public Health, Vol.19*, at https://doi.org/10.3390/ijerph191912439 (accessed on the 31st of March 2023).

Carole P. Ryan. (1995). "Work isn't what it used to be: Implications, recommendations and strategies for vocational rehabilitation". *Journal of Rehabilitation*, Vol. 61.

Chandler K., White B. and Willmott L. (2018). "Safeguarding Rights to Liberty and Security where People with Disability are Subject to Detention and Restraint: A Rights-based Approach (Part One)." *Psychiatry Psychology & Law, Vol. 9;25(3).*

Edna M. Szymanski & Henry T. Trueba. (1994). "Castification of people with disabilities: Potential disempowering aspects of classification in disability services." *Journal of Rehabilitation, 60.*

Emma L. McKinney, Victor McKinney, & Leslie Swartz. (2021). "Access to healthcare for people with disabilities in South Africa: Bad at any time, worse during COVID-19?" *South African Family Practice, Vol. 63(1),* p. 1 at htts://doi.org/10.4102/safp.v63i1.5226 (accessed on the 31st of March 2023)

Eric Badu. (2016)."Access Barriers to Health Care among People with Disabilities in the Kumasi Metropolis of Ghana". *Canadian Journal of Disability Studies, VOL. 5 No. 2.*

Francesco Seatzu. (2020). "Empowering Persons with Disabilities: Socio-Economic Rights as a Pathway to Personal Autonomy and Independence". *Northwestern Journal of Human Rights, Vol.18,* Issue 2, a <https://scholarlycommons.law.northwestern.edu/njihr/vol18/iss2/2> (accessed on the 9th of May 2023).

Francesco Seatzu. (2020). "Empowering Persons with Disabilities: Socio-Economic Rights as a Pathway to Personal Autonomy and Independence". *Northwestern Journal of Human Rights Vol. 18.* At <https://scholarlycommons.law.northwestern.edu/njihr/vol18/iss2/2> (accessed on the 5th of September 2022)

Francesco Seatzu. (2020). "Empowering Persons with Disabilities: Socio-Economic Rights as a Pathway to Personal Autonomy and Independence." *Northwestern Journal of Human Rights, Vol. 18, Issue 2,* at <https://schol

Mall S and Swartz L. (2012). "Sexuality, disability and human rights: Strengthening healthcare for disabled people". *South African Medical Journal. Vol. 102(10).*

Michelle Fine, and Adrienne Asch. (1981). "Disabled Women: Sexism without the Pedestal." *Journal of Sociology and Social Welfare Vol.* 8.

Ofuani A. Irene. (2011). "The right to economic empowerment of persons with disabilities in Nigeria: How enabled?". *African Human Rights Law Journal, Vol 11 No.*

Theses and Dissertations

1. Angelo Dube, Protection of the Rights of Persons Living with Disabilities under the African Human Rights System Masters Dissertation in Human Rights and Democratisation in Africa, the University of Pretoria, 2007, at: https://www.researchgate.net/publication/242235445 (accessed on the 27th of September 2022)
2. Ayesha Roomaney. Assessing the Right to Physical Access to Justice for Persons with Disabilities. Masters Dissertation, Faculty of Law, University of Western Cape, South Africa, 2017.
3. Bolima S. Ambang, Socio-Legal Protection of the Vulnerable Group under International Law: Case Study of the Elderly, Ph.D Thesis, University of Soa, Faculty of Law and Political Science, (Unpublished).
4. Chavia Ali, Forgotten Victims of Armed Conflict: Challenges Faced by Persons With Disabilities, Masters Thesis in International Human Rights Law, Faculty of Law, Lund University, Sweden, 2017.
5. Mary F. Tukov. The Education of Children with Special Needs in Cameroon: The Role of Teachers and Parents towards Inclusive Education. Master Dissertation in Special Needs Education. Department of Special Needs Education, Faculty of Education, University of Oslo Norway, 2008.
6. Tukov M.F., The education of children with special needs in Cameroon: The role of teachers and parents towards inclusive education, unpublished Masters dissertation in Special Needs Education, University of Oslo, 2008.

Reports

Alice Priddy, 2019, Disability and Armed Conflict. The Geneva Academy of International Humanitarian Law and Human Rights, Academy Briefing No. 14.

Department of Social Development. White Paper on the Rights of Persons with Disabilities, Government Gazette, South Africa, 2016, at www.gpwonline.co.za (accessed on the 5th of September 2022)

Eilionóir Flynn *et al.* Access to Justice of Persons with Disabilities. Report of the Centre for Disability Law and Policy, 2019.

Eva J.E Mayer. Study on the Rights of Persons with Disabilities in Cameroon. Report at the African Union of the Blind (AFUB) and the Cameroon

National Association for the Blind (CNAB) in partnership with Disability Rights Promotion International (DRPI) and Swedish Association of the Visually Impaired (SRF), 2007.

Friedrich Ebert Stiftung, Vulnerability in Cameroon's Conflict Regions Causes, manifestations and consequences on the population, report of Friedrich Ebert Stiftung, Yaoundé, Cameroun, Presses Universitairesd"Afrique, 2020.

Gerard Quinn *et al.* Human rights and disability. Summary report to the Office of the UN High Commissioner on Human Rights (OHCHR), 2002.

Human Rights Watch, Report Submitted to the UN Special Rapporteur on the Rights of Persons with Disabilities regarding Persons with Disabilities in the Context of Armed Conflict, June 2021.

International LabourOrganisation. 1998. *Vocational rehabilitation and employment of disabled persons: General survey on the Reports of the Vocational Rehabilitation and Employment (Disabled Persons) Convention (No. 159) and Recommendation (No. 168), 1983.* Report III (Part 1B) of the Committee of Experts on the Application of Conventions and Recommendations, International Labour Conference, 86th session, Geneva, 1998 (Geneva).

Mark Simpson, Gráinne McKeever and Anne Marie Gray. Social security systems based on dignity and respect Equality and Human Rights Commission research report. 2017.p. 29 at www.equalityhumanrights.com (accessed on the 31st of March 2023)

Michael Chege. Political parties in East Africa: Diversity in political party systems. Report prepared for the International Institute for Democracy and Electoral Assistance (IDEA), 2007, p. 7 https://www.oozebap.org/biblio/pdf/PP_East_Africa_Web.pdf (accessed on the 1st of July 2023)

Nora Groce. (2004). HIV/AIDS and disability: capturing hidden voices: the World Bank/Yale University global survey on HIV/AIDS and disability. Working paper. World Bank, Washington, US.

Raymond Lang & Lucy Upah. Scoping study: Disability issues in Nigeria. report of the DFID, Nigeria. (2008) at http://www.ucl.ac.uk/lc- ccr/downloads/scopingstudies/dfi_nigeriareport (accessed on the 27th of March 2023).

UN-Habitat, "Global Report on Human Settlements 2007: Enhancing Urban Safety and Security" (2007).

United Nations Division for Social Policy Development, Toolkit on Disability for Africa: Inclusive Health Services for Persons with Disabilities.

United States Agency for International Development, "Rights of Persons with Disability in the Armed Conflict in the East of Ukraine". Analytical Report of the Ukrainian Helsinki Human Rights Union, Ukrainian Helsinki Human Rights Union, 2016.

World Health Organization & World Bank. (2011). World report on disability 2011. World Health Organization. https://apps.who.int/iris/handle/10665/44575 (accessed on the 25th of April 2023)

Electronic Sources

http://humanitariandisabilitycharter.org/ (accessed on the 17th of July 2023)

http://www.hrw.org/news/2021/06/08/persons-disabilities-context-arm-conflict (accessed on the 17th of July 2023)

http://www.un.org/development/desa/disabilities/news/dspd/un-security-council/html (accessed on the 17th of July 2023)

https://african.org/empowerment/CONTINENTAL%20PLAN%20OF%20ACTION%20(1999-2009).pdf (accessed on the 27th of August 2023).

https://reliefweb.int/report/world/qa-oau-convention-remains-key-plank-refugee- protectionafricaafter40years?gclid=CjwKCAjwrranBhAEEiwA-zbhNtfSdfw17Fn0K05cdLZXPgaQ8_w_Cu6H3eVL18Fd69CURmob-8mkzShoCMBkQAvD_BwE (accessed on the 29th of August 2023).

https://www.hrw.org/topic/disability-rights (accessed on the 17th of July 2023)

https://www.ohchr.org/en/instruments-mechanisms/instruments/ (accessed on the 26th of 2023)

https://www.right-to-education.org/page/african-framework (accessed on the 10th of March 2023)

https://www.studycountry.com/guide/CM-education.htm (accessed on the 1st of December 2022)

https://www.studycountry.com/guide/CM-education.htm (accessed on the 1st of December 2022)

https://www.un.org/development/desa/disabilities/disability-laws-and-acts-by-country- area.html (accessed on the 26th of 2023)

https://www.un.org/disabilities/documents/convention/convention_accessible_pdf.pdf (accessed on the 18th of July 2023)

https://www.un.org/en/content/disabilitystrategy/assets/documentation/UN_Disability_Inclusion_Strategy_english.pdf (accessed on the 18th of July 2023)

https://www.unhcr.org/news/news/qa-oau-convention-remains-key-plank-refugee- protection-africa-after-40-years (accessed on the 29th of August 2023).

U.N. General Assembly, Social, Humanitarian, & Cultural ,available at http://www.un.org/ga/61/third/third.shtml. Accessed July 2020.

World Health Organization, The Toronto Declaration on the Global Prevention of Elder Abuse, 32 (2002), http://www.who.int/ageing/projects/elder_abuse/alc_toronto_declaration_en.pdf. (Accessed August 2019).

U.N. Economic and Social Council, Substantive Session of 2012: Report of the High Commissioner for Human Rights, 33, U.N. Doc. E/2012/51 (Apr. 20, 2012), availlableathttp://www.un.org/ga/search/view_doc.asp?symbol=E/2012/51. Accessed, 20 May 2023.

General Assembly resolution 61/106, annex I. UN General Assembly, Convention on the Rights of Persons with Disabilities: resolution/ adopted by the General Assembly, A/RES/ 61/106, (Acessed 24th January 2007) available at http://www.refworld.org/docid/45f973632.html. Convention on the Rights of Persons with Disabilities, 2515 U.N.T.S. 3. (May 3, 2022)

UN Human Rights Council, Report of the Special Rapporteur on Adequate Housing as a Component of the Right to an Adequate Standard of Living, and on the Right to Non-Discrimination in This Context, Miloon Kothari: addendum: mission to Canada A/HRC/10/7/Add.3, (9 to 22 Oct. 2007), (Feb. 17 2009) available at http://www.refworld.org/docid/49b7af2c2.htm, accessed on 12th of June 2022.

UN Human Rights Council, Report of the Special Rapporteur on the Right of Everyone to the Enjoyment of the Highest Attainable Standard of Physical and Mental Health, Anand Grover, A/HRC/11/12, (Mar. 31 2009) available at http://www.refworld.org/docid/49faf7652.html;

Report of the Special Rapporteur on the Right of Everyone to the Enjoyment of the Highest Attainable Standard of Physical and Mental Health: A/HRC/7/11, 31 at 42 (Jan. 2022) http://www.who.int/medicines/areas/human_rights/A_HRC_7_11.pdf

UN Human Rights Council, UN Human Rights Council: Addendum to the Report of the Special Rapporteur on the Situation of Human Rights and Fundamental Freedoms of Indigenous People, Study Regarding Best Practices Carried out to Implement the Recommendations Contained in the Annual Reports of the Special Rapporteur, A/HRC/4/32/Add.4, (Feb. 26 2007), available at <http://www.refworld.org/docid/4623896f2.html> accessed on the 15th of December 2020)

U.N. Secretary General, Second Review and Appraisal of the Madrid International Plan of Action on Ageing, E/CN.5/2012/5 78, (Nov. 3 2022) available at http://daccess-ddsny.un.org/doc/UNDOC/GEN/N11/579/60/PDF/N1157960.pdf?Open Element

U.N. Committee on Economic, Social and Cultural Rights (CESCR), General

Comments, available at <http://tbinternet.ohchr.org/_layouts/treatybody external/TBSearch.aspx?Lang=en&TreatyID=9&DocTypeID=11> (accessed on the 20th of Febuary 2022).

Women and Armed Conflict Global commitmentshttp://www.un.org/womenwatch/daw/beijing/beijingat10/E.%20Women%20and%20armed%20conflict%20(Sep%2009).pdf.

HelpAge Intl. Psychosocial support for older carers: a summary, 2011. 1 available 17.atwww.helpage.org.

Centers for Disease Control and Prevention & National Center for Health Statistics, Health, United States, 2013, With Special Feature on Prescription Drugs 178 (2013), available at http://www.cdc.gov/nchs/data/hus/hus13.pdf#052 [perma.cc/77HR-LNN7]. (Accessed March 2020).